EDUCATION AND VALUES IN THE MAHABHARATA

The Author

Dr. N. L. Gupta (*b*. 1940-) is the first scholar to obtain a Ph.D. from two different faculties of Nagpur University. He has many firsts to his credit. He is the first candidate to submit a thesis for D. Litt. in R.S. University, Raipur. He is the first writer to get subsidy for a Hindi book from the Governor of Mahabharata.

Dr. Gupta is a prolific writer. Besides many research papers, he has authored twentytwo books in both Hindi and English. After serving for three years in a Degree College, Dr. Gupta joined the Kendriya Vidyalaya Sangathan, New Delhi, in 1965. Presently, he is working as Assistant Commissioner, Kendriya Vidyalaya Sangathan (Delhi Region), New Delhi.

Education and Values in the Mahabharata

DR. N.L. GUPTA, D.Litt.
Assistant Commissioner
Kendriya Vidyalaya Sangathan,
(Delhi Region), New Delhi

CONCEPT PUBLISHING COMPANY, NEW DELHI - 110059

ISBN 81-7022-567-1

First Published 1995

Published and Printed by
Ashok Kumar Mittal
Concept Publishing Company
A/15-16, Çommercial Block, Mohan Garden
NEW DELHI - 110059 (India)

Foreword

Of the two great Sanskrit epics of India, the Mahabharata is one, the other being Ramayana. The word 'Bharata' signifies 'battle of the Bharatas' and the word 'Mahabharata', means the great narrative of the 'battle of the Bharatas'. Divided into 18 Parvas or 'Books', it consists of over 1,00,000 shlokas including those of its supplement, known as Harivamsha. The epic available in two recensions, the Northern and Southern and further sub-divided into versions according to the scripts in which the text is written, has been edited and collated by the Bhandarkar Oriental Research Institute, Pune.

About the contents of the Mahabharata, it is a great national epic and men and women, young and old, rich and poor, high and low, simple and sophisticated, all derive entertainment, inspiration and guidance from it. The well-known literary works in most of the Indian languages, the popular folk-songs and ballads sung by the itinerant bards, draw their inspiration from it. There is indeed no sphere of Indian life, private or public, which is not deeply influenced by this great epic; this is mainly due to the encyclopaedic character of the epic. It is said that in the fields of Dharma (religion and ethics) Artha (material sciences), Kama (Pleasure of life), and Moksha (Spiritual emancipation), whatever is taught in this epic may be found elsewhere, but whatever is not found in it, will not be found anywhere.

It is this vast treasure of knowledge that Dr. N.L. Gupta, a scholar in himself, has tried to dig and discover the gems found in the sphere of education and values in the Mahabharata. Under the headings of various topics and the aims of education, educational institutions, teacher-taught relationship, the subjects of education, value-system, methods of teaching, examinations, etc. Dr. Gupta has culled material from this epic of vast magnitude. Quoting profusely from the original epic, he has provided us with an exhaustive account of branches of learning then prevalent and the masters of learnings as mentioned in the epic. Dr. Gupta's treatise is important in this sense also as the education in the Mahabharata holds equally good for the age preceding this epic since the Mahabharata is a good record of what had prevailed earlier. It is also a good testimony of what happened after the Mahabharata age as the system prevalent in that age continued for a long period and in some cases is current upto the modern times as is seen in the Sanskrit Pathshalas.

The book is illuminating and can be studied with profit by students and teachers and scholars and researchers.

A great scholar of Sanskrit, Ancient Indian History and Hindi, as Dr. Gupta, is, I congratulate him on producing this valuable and brilliant work. I am sure it would be widely read by all concerned.

(Prof.) Ganga Ram Garg, M.A., Ph.D.,
Former Vice-chancellor,
Gurukula Kangri Vishwavidyalaya, Hardwar &
Editor, Encyclopaedia of the Hindu World, International Encyclopaedia of Indian Literature, Concise Oxford Companion to Hindi Literature, World perspectives on Swami Dayanand Sarasvati, etc.

II/20 Vanaprastha Ashram,
Jwalapur (Hardwar) 249407
November 16, 1994

Preface

In the present study educational data as visualized in the Mahabharata has been analysed at length and certain conclusions put forth in a scientific manner. For this purpose, the *Critical Edition* of the Epic published by the Bhandarkar Oriental Research Institute, Pune, has been used. Besides seven appendices, there are in all twelve chapters.

Chapter I is introductory in which the nature, extent, significance, time, etc., of the Epic have been clearly delineated. Chapter II deals with the stratification of the then society and its implications for the system of education. It also highlights the contribution of the warrior class in general and the scholar kings in particular towards the advancement of various branches of learning.

Chapter III contains the nature and extent of curriculum characterizing its various salient features. Chapter IV deals with various types of occupations and vocations including training in arms, warcrafts, science of medicine and surgery, various crafts and fine arts. A list of 64 Kalas with a brief explanation of the technical terms also finds place in this chapter.

Stating the role of "Dharma" in the area of Education and Aims of Religious Education, a new concept of Moral and Religious Education has been presented in Chapter V. In the context of the contents of the Epic, our moral, social, cultural and spirtual values have been analysed critically. In Chapter VI, under the sub-heading "Two Sets of Principles", Yug Dharmà and Sanatan Dharma have been explained, which obviously stand for the changeable and eternal sets of values. Various dimensions of value-creating education have also been analysed. Many modes and methods, tools and techniques practised in the ancient system of education for inculcating moral, cultural and spiritual values have also been critically examined. Righteousness is the quintessence of "Sanatana Dharm". To confine "Dharma" to one particular faith is negation of "Dharma" as fundamental values are common in all the religions of the world. Notwithstanding this "Dharma" eschews the religious doctrines of different creeds and sects. The Mahabharata explains in diverse ways the broad and enduring outlook "Dharma" provides us. It is the firm conviction of Maharishi Vyas that "Artha" and "Kama" can be had through Dharma. But due to deviation from the path of Dharma a value crisis has emerged as a global phenomenon. Therefore, the Mahabharata declares firmly, "Righteousness, thy name is victory" (Yto Dharmastato Jayah). Chapter VII deals with the entire gamut of the perception. There is no gainsaying the fact that the value-system as visualized in the Mahabharata is very complex and at times rather self-contradictory. But this self-contradiction is because of the very character of the epic. It is not an epic of art like the Ramayana, but an epic of growth, wherein there had been profuse interpolations from time to time. In spite of all odds and conflicting views "Dharma" stands as victor. In Chapter VIII status of women has been critically examined from the educational point of view. Special stress has been laid on the informal type of education, which was the order of the day.

Chapter IX deals with five types of centres of learning, *i.e.* hermitages, parishads or samiti, royal assemblies, sites of sacrifices (Yajnya Mandapas) and places of pilgrimage. Highlighting the indispensability of the teacher and his personal impact on the studies and conduct of the pupils, various subtle aspects of teachership and studentship have been analysed in Chapter X on the basis of data available in the Mahabharata. Prominent aspects like Gurudakshina and exhortation by the preceptor have been dealt with in detail.

Chapter XI presents life sketches constructed from the material available in the epic and other allied sources in respect of the prominent masters of learning (Acharyas) including the great sage Vyas and his disciples, Kulpati Shaunak, disciples of Shaunak, Lomharshan and Ugrashrava, Maharishi Narada, Uddhava, Bhishma, Dronacharya, Shukracharya, etc. Chapter XII is the concluding chapter. To make the work more useful six appendices have been given at the end of the book including a short bibliography of the works referred to.

I shall deem my effort fruitful if this monograph inspires some scholars for further research for which there is a vast scope. It is a well-known fact that we have abundant literature highlighting the cultural history of educational ideals and institutions of the Western world, but there are very few on Asian traditions. For reconstruction of the history of education, it is essential to present profound studies of the underlying educational philosophy in various educational traditions.

I express my deep sense of gratitude to Dr. Ganga Ram Garg, former Vice-chancellor Gurukula Kangri Vishwavidyalaya and a scholar of international repute for having lent a foreword to this work.

I am thankful to Shri Ashok K. Mittal of CONCEPT who readily agreed to publish the present monograph and brought it out in record time with a get-up befitting the reputation of the publishing house. Last but not least my sincere thanks are due to Shri Jaswant Rai Mittal who inspired me to be associated with CONCEPT.

"Buddha Purnima"
May 25, 1994,
C-1/23, Airport Authority Housing Complex,
Mahipalpur, New Delhi-110037

DR. N. L. GUPTA

Contents

1

Introduction

Mahabharata (Mbh.) : Etymology

According to Panini "Bharata" signifies "the battle of the Bharata" and as such the Mahabharata means "the great narrative of the battle of the Bharatas" as explained by Winternitz.[1] From the internal evidence we come to know that the work is called Mahabharata on account of its greatness, enormity of size and weightiness, which suggest that it outweighs the Veda and other sacred literature of India.[2] According to the meaning of one of the readings[3] it is called Mahabharata on account of its greatness and Indianness.

Significance

The Mahabharata is the biggest among the world's epics. It contains one hundred thousand shlokas or verses. Some prose pieces are also there, which pertain to a later period, according to Oldenberg.[4] It is a national ethical code, which has influenced the heritage of arts, literature, culture, religion and social phenomena since the dawn of civilizations. It is not only an emotional treasure of Indian life but also an encyclopaedia of our composite culture. It is a shastra or manual of ethics, social and political philosophy. It deals with all the four aims of human life — Dharma (righteousness), Artha (economy), Kama (pleasure) and Moksha (salvation). Dharma includes moral, social, cultural and spiritual values. Artha deals with material or worldly prosperity. Pleasures pertaining to the mundane life are Kama, the main aim of which, according to the Hindu ideal, was to maintain the line of one's progeny. Moksha, the ultimate aim of life, deals with emancipation of the self from the meshes of the world. All the six systems of Indian philosophy opine identically in this regard. Therefore, the statement of the epic itself—that whatever is incorporated here may be found elsewhere; but what is not found here cannot be got anywhere else[5] is no exaggeration; nor can the saying that "Vyas has touched every subject under the sun" be challenged. (व्यासोच्छिष्टम् जगत्सर्वम्)

R.C. Dutta has rightly observed : "No work in Europe, not Homer in Greece nor Virgil in Italy, not Shakespeare and Milton in English-speaking lands, is the national property of the same extent as the epics of India are to the Hindus. No single work excepting the Bible has such influence in affording moral instructions in Christian lands as the *Mahabharata* and the *Ramayana* in India. No work of imagination could be named, always excepting the *Iliad*, as so rich and so true as the *Mahabharata*—not in torment and suffering as in Dante, not in overwhelming passions as in Shakespeare—but in human character in its calm dignity of strength and repose, like those immortal figures in marble which the ancients turned out, and which modern sculptors have vainly sought to reproduce."

Extent of Mahabharata

The Mahabharata is said to comprise one lakh shlokas, which indicates that by that time it had earned fame as a "treatise of one lac verses" (Shatsahasri Samhita). Bharat and Mahabharat have been mentioned independently in Ashvalayan Grhya Sutra which is indicative of their separate identity.[6] According to Dr. V.S. Agrawala[7] by the Shunga period Bharat had got merged into greater Mahabharat. Mahabharata[8] also admits that in due course Bharat itself, incorporating various episodes, came into being as Mahabharata. Being an "Epic of Growth" it was but natural that with the span of time the process of interpolation also continued. This process of enlargement and refinement is indicative of the fact that the epic played an important role in the then society because of its rich cultural content and as such it could not be overlooked.[9]

The entire epic is divided into 18 sections (parvans), and each parvan is further divided into several sub-sections (sub-parvans). The number of chapters and verses included in chapter are mentioned in the text of the Mahabharata itself. Here, in Table 1.1 we are showing a comparison between the number of chapters and shlokas mentioned in the text of the Mahabharata and actually found in the Critical Edition (BORI, Pune) of the Mahabharata, which has been used for the present study.

Table 1.1 : The number of chapters and verses in the text of the Mahabharata and as actually found in the Critical Edition (BORI, Pune).

S. No.	Parvan (Section)	As mentioned in Mahabharata		As actually available in the Critical Edition	
		Chapters	No. of Verses	Chapters	No. of Verses
1.	Adi	227	8884	218	7984
2.	Sabha	78	2511	72	2811
3.	Van	269	11664	269	11664
4.	Virat	67	2067	67	2050
5.	Udyog	185	6698	186	6698
6.	Bhishma	117	5884	117	5884
7.	Drona	170	8909	170	8909
8.	Karn	69	4968	69	4900
9.	Shalya	59	3220	59	3220
10.	Sauptik	18	870	18	870
11.	Stree	27	775	27	775
12.	Shanti	329	14632	339	14525
13.	Anushashan	143	8000	154	7793
14.	Ashvamedhik	103	3320	133	3320
15.	Ashramvaslk	42	1505	42	1505
16.	Mausal	8	320	8	300
17.	Mahapristhanik	3	320	3	120
18.	Swargarohan	5	209	5	200
	Total	2082	84853	1956	83136

Sub-Parvan of Mahabharata

Here it will not be out of place to give the particulars of sub-parvans of the above parvans as given in Table 1.1. It will help grasp the contents of the epic and facilitate readers to know its story. The following are the sub-parvans :

(i) *Adi-Parvan* : 18 sub-parvan : (1) Story of Paushya, (2) Story of Paulomi, (3) Episode of Astik, (4) Genealogy, (5) Birth of Pandavas, (6) Burning of Wax house, (7) Hidimba, (8) Assassination of Bakasur, (9) Meeting Chitraratha, (10) Draupadi Swayamvar, (11) Marriage, (12) Advent of Vidur, (13) Acquiring a separate kingdom, (14) Pilgrimage of Arjuna, (15) Abduction of Subhadra, (16) Wedding—Presents by Krishna, (17) Khandaw forest on fire and (18) Advent of the demon Maya (Mayasur) who prepared the celestial mandap for the Pandvas).

(ii) *Sabha Parvan* : 9 sub-parvans : (1) Construction of palatial court (Sabha-bhavan), (2) Counselling for royal supremacy (Chakravarty-pad), (3) Assassination of Jarasandha, (4) Conquering the world

(Digvijaya), (5) Rajsuya Yajnya, (6) Arghya-dan, (7) Murder of Shishupal, (8) Gambling (second time) and (9) Religious Bath (Avbhrit Snan).

(iii) *Van-Parvan* : 22 sub-parvan : (1) Kirmir-vadh, (2) Departure of Arjuna, (3) Duet of Arjuna with Kirat, (4) Reaching of Arjuna in Indralok, (5) Nala Episode, (6) Pilgrimage by the Pandavas, (7) Murder of Jatasur, (8) Duet with Yaksha, (demi-god), (9) Duet with Nivtkavach, (10) Meeting with Nagraja, (11) Problem of Markandey, (12) Conversation between Draupadi and Satyabhama, (13) Abduction of the cattle, (14) Seeing deer in dream by Yudhisthir, (15) Vrihidronik, (16) Abduction of Draupadi, (17) Release of Jayadrath, (18) Episode of Ram, (19) Eulogizing chastity of Savitri, (20) Parting with ear-rings (Kundalas), (21) Arney (pertaining to Arni, a holy stick) and (22) Aindradyumna.

(iv) *Virata Parvan* : 5 sub-parvan : (1) Entry of the Pandavas in the capital of Virata, (2) Observing the condition of exile, (3) Murder of Kichaka, (4) Abduction of cows and (5) Marriage of Uttara.

(v) *Udyoga Parvan* : 11 sub-parvan : (1) Accumulation of army, (2) Proceeding of Sanjay, (3) Insomnia of Dhritrashtra, (4) Sanatsujat, (5) Moment of Farewell, (6) Departure of Lord Krishna to Hastinapur for arbitration, (7) March of the armies, (8) Going of Owl Messenger, (9) Rath pilgrimage, (10) Episode of Amba and (11) Dispute between Bhishma and Karna.

(vi) *Bhishma Parvan* : 5 sub-parvan : (1) Coronation of Bhishma, (2) Geography of Jamboo Dwip, (3) Description of extent of Jamboo Dwip, (4) Bhagavadgeeta and (5) Death of Bhishma.

(vii) *Drona Parvan* : 8 sub-parvan : (1) Coronation of Drona, (2) Assassination of Samsaptaka, (3) Murder of Abhimanyu, (4) Vow of Arjuna, (5) Murder of Jayadrath; (6) Ghatotkach, (7) Murder of Drona and (8) Use of Narayana weapon.

(viii) *Karna-Parvan.*

(ix) *Shalya-Parvan* : 4 sub-parvan : (1) Murder of Shalya, (2) Hiding of Duryodhana in the tank, (3) Duet (between Bhima and Duryodhana) and (4) Sarswat.

(x) *Sauptik Parvan* : 2 sub-parvan : (1) Sauptik (2) Aishik.

(xi) *Stri-Parvan* : 3 sub-parvan : (1) Tarpan of the corpses, (2) Mourning of women and (3) Shraddha.

(xii) *Shanti-Parvan* : 6 sub-parvan : (1) Duties of a King, (2) King's duties in odd situations, (3) Moksha-parvan, (4) Coronation of Dharmraj (Yudhisthir) and (5) Grihvibhajan.

(xiii) *Anushashan Parvan* : 2 sub-parvan : (1) Dandharma and (2) Move of Bhishma towards heaven.

(xiv) *Ashvamedhik Parvan* : 2 sub-parvan : (1) Ashvamedh sacrifice and (2) Anugeeta.
(xv) *Ashramwasik Parvan* : 3 sub-parvan : (1) Dhritrashtra's resort to forest, (2) Son's vision and (3) Advent of Narada.
(xvi) *Mausal Parvan*
(xvii) *Mahapristhanik*
(xviii) *Swargarohan Parvan*

Interpolations in Mahabharata

In fact the old heroic poem, dealing with the bloody family feud resulting in the overthrow of the Kauravas by the Pandavas, forms the nucleus of Mahabharata, which was originally called Jaya containing only eight thousand eight hundred verses. Shorenson, who made Mahabharata his life's work and study, attempted reconstruction of the Epic in 1883. According to him, in its oldest form, it was a saga, and the creation of a single mind, which had no contradiction, repetition, digression. By elimination of interpolations Shorenson declared the original genuine epic to contain only eight thousand shlokas.

This nucleus assumed the present form of Mahabharata, in due course, by periodical additions of different types of matter as the following :

(a) Legendary matter from the bardic repertoire having but a casual connection, in certain cases, with the epic heroes;
(b) Myths and legends of Brahmanical origin and didactic sections pertaining to Brahmanical philosophy, ethics and law stressing the superiority of the Brahmanas;
(c) Cosmological, genealogical and geographical matter in the nature of the Puranas and local myths;
(d) Myths of Vishnu and later of Shiva;
(e) Ascetic poetry; and
(f) Prose pieces and Brahmanical legends and moral tales, entirely or partly in prose.

Of the heroic legends the episodes of Shakuntala, Yayati, Nahusha, Nala and Damyanti, and Rama are well known. Shanti parvan (Section XII) and Anushashan parvan (Section XIII) are repositories of religion and philosophy, various lores and arts and so on. "The inclusion of this diverse matter, which has made the Mahabharata at once a Kavya,

Shashtra, Shruti, Law, Philosophy, etc., indicates the uniform popularity of the great Epic through the ages and the anxiety of the compilers to make the Mahabharata encyclopaedia for all time".[10]

Three Beginnings of Mahabharata

The editors of the *Critical Edition* (BORI, Pune) of the Mahabharata have established linkages between the three beginnings and three editions of Mahabharata, *i.e.* Jaya, Bharata and Mahabharata. As the nomenclatures reveal the "Jaya" had been the original form of Mahabharata cited by Vyas which marks victory of Pandavas over Kauravas. The epic itself speaks of its three different beginnings in the following stanza :

मन्वादि भारतं केचिदास्तिकादि तथापरे ।
तथोपरिचराद्यन्ये विप्राः सम्यगधीयते ।।

(The epic is studied by the scholars with three different beginnings—some from "Manvadi", some from "Astikadi", while others from "Uparicharadi")

Thus there are these three beginnings of the Mahabharata :

(i) Manvadi, *i.e.* from the very beginning of the extent after the mangal-sloka "नारायणं नमस्कृत्य", etc., according to the *Critical Edition*, followed by the conversation between Sauti (or Suta, etc.) and the sages at Saunaka's hermitage;
(ii) Astikadi, *i.e.* from the description of Janamejaya's Sarpasatra, where begins the Astika-parvan; and
(iii) Uparicharadi, *i.e.* from the commencement of the actual narration of the history of the Bharatas, where begins the Amsavatara-parvan.

Thus correlation of the beginning and the narrator, etc., can be easily understood from Table 1.2.

Table 1.2 : Correlation of beginning and narrator.

Beginning	S. no. of Ch. in Adi Parvan (Beginning point)	Cited by	Nomenclature of Edition	No. of Shlokas contained in the Edition
Uparicharadi	54th Ch.	Vyas	Jaya	8800
Astikadi	13th Ch.	Vaishampayan	Bharata	24000
Manvadi	1st Ch.	Suta	Mahabharata	100000

Interpreting one shloka in his own way, Dr. P.P.S. Shastri observed that the commutation of the Mahabharata is one hundred thousand shlokas, if counted along with narratives, and only twentyfour thousand, if these are excluded.

Time of Mahabharata

As we have already mentioned that being the Epic of growth Mahabharata had different shapes at different times. The development of the Epic in its present shape shown by Hopkins is as follows :

> 400 B.C. : There is a collection of Bharata lays, in which the Pandavas are yet unknown.
> 400-200 B.C. : There springs up a Mahabharata tale, in which the Pandavas are the heroes and Krishna is a demi-god.
> 300 B.C. to 100 or 200 A.D. : Krishna now becomes the all-god; Interpolations of a didactic nature; new episodes added.
> 200-400 A.D. : The introduction and later books are added.

With regard to the date of the Mahabharata. Winternitz concludes that "the Mahabharata cannot have received its present form earlier than the 4th century B.C. and later than the 4th century A.D.".[12] The orthodox opinion, however, is that the war took place in 3101 B.C. calculating on the basis of the generally accepted belief in India that in 1899 A.D. five thousand years had elapsed since the beginning of the Kali Age. We agree with this orthodox opinion.[13]

Is Mahabharata Historical or Allegorical ?

The great question is : Is the Mahabharata historical or allegorical ? Mahatma Gandhi tells us on this point that ever since he was first acquainted with Sir Edwin Arnold's translation of the Bhagavadgita, called "The Song Celestial", in 1888-89, he had felt that it was not a historical work. "I do not regard the Mahabharata", he tells us, "as a historical work in the accepted sense of the term". This does not mean that the persons in the Mahabharata are not historical; but the many situations, speeches, dialogues, interpretations, conclusions and so forth need not necessarily be regarded as historical. They are what the great Vyasa has put into the mouths of the great actors. Mahatma Gandhi advances three arguments for regarding the Mahabharata as allegorical rather than historical:

First, that the Adi-parvan contains a very powerful evidence in support of his (Gandhi's) statement. Vyasa ascribes to many of the heroes of the Mahabharata either subhuman or superhuman origins. These cannot be regarded as historical in any sense. For example, he tells us Bhishma was born from the Ganga, Karna from the sun, Dharma from the God of Death, Bhima from the wind and Agastaya from a pitcher. Who can say that these actors or anything connected with them may be regarded in any sense as historical?

Secondly, as Mahadev Desai has put it, it is permissible to poets, dramatists and historians to ascribe imaginary characters to historical persons. For example, we may see how the great Shakespeare painted Richard III as a diabolical being.

"So misshapen and sent before my time into the world, that dogs bark at me when I halt by them".

Thucydides, the great historian who has, by general consent been regarded as a very conscientious historian, has not hesitated to introduce imaginary dialogues or to invent speeches for his characters in order to elucidate different situations. Thucydides has himself told us that he has deliberately done so in order that the lesson might be well impressed upon the minds of his readers.

Thirdly, if the Mahabharata is interpreted more in an allegorical than in a historical sense, then the Bhagavadgita itself might be taken to represent the moral duel that is perpetually going on inside us. Historical names have been introduced by the author of the great epic only to drive home some ethical and religious principles. For example, the Pandavas were regarded as the forces of light, the Kauravas of darkness and the Kurukshetra as the human body in which they played their part. Arjuna and Krishna might themselves allegorically be taken to represent the "individual ego and the great In-dweller".

In this way, according to Mahatma Gandhi, we have to interpret both the Mahabharata and the Bhagavadgita more in an allegorical than in historical sense.

In spite of certain contradictory conclusions put forth by the reputed scholars including D.C. Sircar and H.D. Sankaliya challenging the traditional historicity of the Mahabharata with archaeological points of view, the historicity of the main plot and characters cannot be denied. The Epic may be taken as history in a poetic frame, wherein all sorts of exaggerations, symbolism and other poetic elements are bound to prevail; but due to these poetic elements the very historicity of the main story and characters cannot be refuted.

Footnotes

1. *History of Indian Literature* Vol. 1, p. 317.
2. चत्वारो एकतो वेदा भारतं चैकमेकतः ।
समागतैः सुरर्षिभिस्तुलामारोपितं पुरा ।।
महत्त्वे गुरुत्वे च ध्रियमाणं ततोऽधिकम् ।
महत्त्वाद्भारवत्वाच्च महाभारतमुच्यते ।।
3. भारतानां महज्जन्म महाभारतमित्युत ।
निरुक्तस्य यो वेद सर्वपापैः प्रमुच्यते ।।
4. *Das Mahabharata*, p. 21.
5. यदिहास्ति तदन्यत्र यन्नेहास्ति न तत्क्वचित् । (Adi 56.33)
6. Utgikar, "Mahabharata in the Asvalayan Grihya Sutra", Proceedings of the First Oriental Conference, Pt II, p. 60.
7. भारत सावित्री, भाग, पृ. २
8. इदं शतसहस्रं तु श्लोकानां पुण्यकर्मणाम् ।
उपाख्यानैः सह ज्ञेयमाद्यं भारतमुत्तमम् ।।
Adi, Ch. I
9. For details please see, V. S. Sukathankar, *The Bhrigus and the Bharat*, ABORI, Vol. 18, pp. 15-76.
10. Dr. A. D. Pusalkar, *Studies in the Epics and Puranas*, p. 4.
11. चतुर्विंशतिसाहस्री चक्रे भारतसंहिताम् ।
उपाख्यानैर्विना तावद् भारतं प्रोच्यते बुधैः ।।
(Adi 1.61)
12. *History of Indian Literature* Vol. 1, p. 465.
13. C. V. Vaidya, *The Mahabharata: A Critique*, p. 50.

2

Social Stratification and Education

Varna-System

Social stratification prevailing during the Mahabharata depicts the picture of a peasant and feudal society in which education remains the privilege of a few, particularly those who could afford it.

Members of royal families and other affluent people could have proper formal and non-formal education in various hermitages or by engaging special tutors who would teach them at home. During the Epic time, Varna and Ashrama were the two most important social institutions.

The entire society was classified into four classes: Brahmin (priest class), Kshatriya (warrior class), Vaishya (merchant class or traders) and Shudra (craftsmen and menial worker). It was assumed that men are not born equally. There are always individual differences which have now been proved psychologically. Personal capacities differ from individual to individual. If a man does work for which he has inborn capacities he can do better as well as derive self-satisfaction. Therefore, it was decided that every man must be asked to do work for which he was best fitted.

Certain assumptions based on this theory have already been refuted by our giant social reformers like Swami Vivekananda and later on by humanists like Jyotiba Fule, B.R. Ambedkar, and Manvendra Nath Roy, the propounder of the theory of "Radical Humanism or Neo-humanism". "Man is the measure for everything" is the pet slogan of these neo-humanists. They do not accept any sort of bondage on man, because it creates stumbling blocks in the way of his progress by limiting his creative talents.

According to them men have an equal right to happiness and this can be realized only by letting them do for which nature has fitted them.

However, society also requires individuals who may put in their best and contribute towards the advancement of society as a whole. Therefore, society was divided into four varnas, as explained above, which was based on the sound principle of "division of labour" because for an all-round development of society, it required the following four classes of people :

(i) The class that gives the society its laws and rules of conduct;
(ii) The class that protects the society and the country at large from external and internal aggression;
(iii) The class that produces food and makes available other necessities of life and helps in the economy of the country;
(iv) The class that can perform menial jobs which may not suit the other three classes.

On the basis of the above classification the varna-system was evolved. Later on it was misunderstood and mistaken and rigidity crept into the system. The mistaken notion came to be known as "caste" which was one of the factors responsible for the degeneration and deterioration of the Indian social phenomena. The Four Varnas went on multiplying into hundreds of castes. Consequently the number of castes, as [illegible] stands today, is more than four thousand in our country.

Duties and Rights of Varnas

Manu[1] says that study, teaching, worshipping, helping others in worshipping, making gifts and accepting gifts are the acts of Brahmins. Three of these six are his means of livelihood. He further says that a Brahmin should abandon all things that are opposed to study and he should teach at all costs. That is the real performance of his duty. He should always study those sciences that augment thinking power, sciences that are useful and works that help the understanding of the Vedas. A similar view has been endorsed by the Mahabharata.[2]

The king was always to be a Kshatriya by varna and the other Kshatriyas had to help the king in the discharge of his duties. Therefore, it was essential on the part of the King to know his duties as prescribed in the scriptures and otherwise. These duties are well expressed in the oath that was supposed to be administered to the kings at their coronation. According to the Mahabharata, the following oath was actually administered to Prithu.

It means that the King had to take an oath again and again that he would protect the Brahma on earth, *i.e.*, the Brahmanas, by thought, word and deed. He would act at any time according to the unchangeable Dharma laid down in the Danda Neeti.

Further the King used to promise that he would not punish the Brahmanas and would protect the whole world from the admixture of the Varnas.

Goutam[3] enjoins that the king should appoint as Purohit (Prime Minister) a Brahman, having knowledge, noble descent, eloquence, august and pleasing appearance, mature and active age and good character, whose rule of life is justice and who abstains from bodily or sensual pleasures. He further mentions that the king should act with his consent. It was presumed that the king acting with the consent of such a purohit prospers and does not get afflicted. In other words every act of the king requires consent of the Purohit just as in England the king requires the consent of the Prime Minister. In this connection, the Mahabharata has also similar views. While lying down on the bed of arrows, Bhishma exhorts Yudhisthir as follows:

> "I shall tell you how and of what kind you should appoint your ministers. Four Brahmanas, learned and honest, who are mature and have completed their study at a teacher's school (that is who are graduates), eight Kshatriyas strong and skilful in the use of weapons, twentyone Vaishyas possessing wealth, three Shudras that are humble and honest in the duties previously mentioned (*i.e.*, the duty of attending upon the other Varnas), and one Suta (by varna) who knows the puranas, has eight qualifications, is fifty years of age, mature and free from jealousy, knows Srutis and Smritis also, is modest and impartial, who is able to control the disputants about any point, who is not greedy of money and who is free form the seven terrific vices. The king should take a decision about anything in the midst of (at least) eight of these ministers and then that decision he should proclaim in his kingdom and should also communicate to the governors of the provinces. In this manner you should govern your subjects".[4]

Similarly it is said that a Vaishya should try his best to increase his wealth by just means, and he should give food to all beings by all his efforts.[5]

Priest Class Vs Warrior Class

Dr. Bhagvatsharan Upaddhyay observes that with the advent of Upnishadic cult the rivalry for supremacy in the arena of knowledge between the priest class and the warrior class had started. The Kshatriyas were prepared to encroach upon the privileges the Brahmanas enjoyed by from the Vedic times. As against ritualism they advocated rationalism and started patronizing profusely the exponents of Atma-vidya. Consequently the Brahmanas also propounded various branches of philosophy. The span of this struggle was quite lengthy stretching down to the 2nd century B.C. and resulted ultimately in the political rise of the priest class. On the one side there were priests like Vashishtha, Parshuram, Katyayan, Turkavsheya, Rakshasa, Patanjali and Pushya Mitra Shunga, etc., on the other were scholar kings who include Vishwamitra, Devapi, Janmejaya, Ashwapati Kaikeya, Prawahan Jaibli, Ajatshatru Kasheya, Janak Videh, Parshwa Mahavir, Buddha, Varihadrath, etc.[6] In the Mahabharata we come across many glimpses of this rivalry, such as between Vashishtha and Vishwamitra, etc. An example of such a rivalry has been elaborated in the Ramayana also.

The details of the struggle that took place between Vashishtha and Vishvamitra over the possession of the divine cow Savala shows that the wealth (specially in cattle) of the asrama excited the king's cupidity; he claimed it on the ground that all treasures belong to the king; on opposition he offered various fabulous substitutes as a price, viz. heaps of silver, 14,000 gold-bedecked elephants, 800 golden four-horsed chariots, 1,000 noble horses, any amount of gold and gems; on continued resistance Vishvamitra took away the "asrama" cattle by force, taking advantage of his privileges as a guest[7] but he was subsequently attacked by mercenary Saka, Yavana, Pahlava and other barbarians employed by the Vasistha asrama, and was forced to flee from his kingdom. Vishvamitra re-issued from his forest refuge and ravaged the Vashishtha monastery, which was burnt and devastated and whence disciples fled by the hundred and thousand. So that for a time it was like a wilderness, but "Vashishtha" rallied the monks and stemmed the Kausika aggression successfully in person; frustrated, king Vishvamitra vowed to become a bierarch himself. This whole episode is nothing but the struggle between the head of a powerful monastery and the king of the land, in which the latter is obliged to bow before heretic influence and prestige, but out of which he emerges successful in a sense, by himself becoming the head of a rival monastic order and institution.

After defeat by Vashishtha and his monks, king Vishvamitra, along with his queen, went to the South, and engaged in Brahman training, where four sons were born to them. After sometime he was recognized in asrama circles as a Kshatriyan teacher (Rajarsi).

Warrior Class and Education

There are numerous references in the Upnishads where the Kshatriyas are represented as the wisest teachers of spiritual knowledge. But it is needless to multiply examples here. In the Mahabharata their accounts are available in several episodes like Sulbhaakhyan, etc. In the history of Hindu religion and philosophy this warrior class enjoyed a very covetous place. The Upnishads mark a new era in the history of human knowledge. This knowledge "did not belong to any Brahmin before, it belonged in all the worlds to the Kshatriya class (warrior class) alone".

From the internal evidences of the Mahabharata, it is obvious that there were mainly two trends of thought in the society—path of knowledge and path of ritualism. The former leads to salvation whereas the latter leads to heaven and involves several rituals described in the Vedas and allied scriptures. The path of knowledge advocated monism and expressly opposed ritualism. The advocates and exponents of this trend were various famous kings such as Videh Janak, Kaikay Ashvapati, Panchal, etc. They used to arrange and patronize various seminars and assemblies of scholars in which elaborate debates (shastrartha) were held in order to affirm and synthesize various currents of thinking about Moksha (salvation) and to open new vistas for further deliberation since "वादे वादे जायते तत्त्वबोध:" True knowledge is obtained through discussion and debate has been our age-old contention. In the Mahabharata it is said that in the palace of Videh Janak about a hundred scholars (sages and other masters of various branches of learning) used to stay every day.[8]

Scholar Kings

There was a good rapport between the priests (purohits) and these scholar kings. To the history of Indian philosophy these scholar-kings have contributed substantially, an account of which is recorded in various Upnishads, particularly the Chhandogya Upnishad. In fact the age of the epic was predominantly the age of sacrifices, when prolonged and expensive sacrifices were performed by the kings. Some of the sacrifices continued even for twelve years, which an ordinary king could not afford. But for the Dwapar age, sacrifice has been mentioned as the noble one.[9]

In the Epic age the rulers were almost from the warrior class. Besides the mastery in using arms and various martial arts they used to have indepth study of the Vedas and other scriptures.

In the Ramayana (I, 80, 27 ff.), the list of subjects the king is expected to study includes Dhanurveda, Veda, Nitisastra and the art (siksha) of elephants and cars, besides the arts of painting (Alekhya), writing (Lekhya), jumping (langhana), and swimming (plavana). In another passage we have mention of writing and numbers (lekhyasamkhya), of fine arts (Gandharvavidya), logic (Nyaya), polity (Nitisastra), etc.

There are several similar lists in the Mahabharata. Reference has already been made to two such lists (XIII, 104, 125; I, ff.)., where we have mentioned Sabdashastram and the sixty-four Kalas together with Yuktisastram (*i.e.* grammar, fine arts and etiquette). Another list enumerates the following (ii, 11, 25): Ashtanga-ayurveda (medicine with its eight branches) Rigveda, Samaveda, Yajurveda, Atharvaveda, Sarvashastrani, Itihasas, Upavedas, Vedangas, Vani of seven kinds, Samas, Shrutisastras (treatises of hymns), various kinds of Gatha literature, Bhashyas (bhashyani tarkayunktani) Natakaa, Kavyas. Kathakhyayikas (Karikah). Hopkins holds the view that probably this list is earlier than the previous one, but both show that "the line of education was away from the Veda and that what time the princes had was given to culture, not to religion".

Hopkins further holds that "as the old royal personal fighting days ended that is, as the princes were more and more expected to be figure-heads in war, and drove into battle to watch it from an elephant's back rather than lead it in a war-car, their older bow-and-sword training was given up; and the time so gained was spent in more effeminate, certainly not more truly intellectual, occupations. Perhaps the late Virata, with the cowardly little crown-prince, shows us the step between."

Requisite Qualities of Kings

According to the Mahabharata[10] the king must be learned, receptive, highly witted, of high calibre. The subjects of studies meant for the kings as mentioned above can easily be visualized in Duryodhana's description of various kings who came to participate in the Rajsuya Sacrifice performed by Yudhishthir, though it is exaggerated but one can find the truth in the following lines—

आर्यास्तु ये वै राजानः सत्यसन्धा महाव्रताः ।
पर्याप्तविद्या वक्तारो वेदावभृथाप्लुताः ।।
धृतिमन्तो ह्रीनिषेधा धर्मात्मानो यशस्विनः ।[11]

From the above, it is clear that the kings were not only fond of various branches of learning but were also experts in selected branches of learning. Venkumar King Prithu had profound scholarship in Veda-vedang, ved of the bow and Dandniti (statecraft[12]) Yudhisthir was expert in vedas, moral religious matters[13] Bhishma was well-versed in several lores including Itihas-puran, spiritual science, Vedas, statecraft, etc.

In Adi parvan (1. 22 ff.) the Pandu princes are described as having studied all the Vedas and the various shastras or treatises on duty, etc. Bhishma was a great scholar of the time. He brought up Dhritrashtra, Pandu and Vidur like his own sons. They are described as being purified by the ceremonies of their order, disciplined by study and the vows and practices of studentship, and emerging into manhood skilled in studies, Veda-vedangas, archery, polity and various martial arts. Pandu excelled in archery and Dhritrashtra in physical strength.

Though many kings were well-versed in Veda-vedangas they never indulged in priesthood, which was the privilege of the Brahmins exclusively. As it has been specified by the law-givers like Manu, "teaching, performing sacrifices for others and receiving gifts" are special to Brahmins similarly "defence or protection of his people" was special to Kshatriyas (the warrior class). According to R.K. Mookerji, "It is also to be noted that such study as was enjoined for a Kshatriya might make him sufficiently proficient in the Veda to be able to teach, and teach a Brahmin student who should not go without education for a failure of a Brahmin teacher. Thus, normally, the Kshatriya was only to study, and the Brahmin to study as also to teach and perform sacrifices for others. It is thus evident that the study as a qualification of teaching and direction of religious practices will be different in scope and method from that which is followed by occupations not directly depending on or connected with it".[14]

Footnotes

1. अध्यापनमध्ययनं यजनं याजनं तथा।
दानं प्रतिग्रहश्चैव षट्कर्माण्यग्रजन्मनः।।
षण्णां तु कर्मणामस्य त्रीणि कर्माणि जीविका।
— Manu X, 75-76
सर्वान् परित्यजेदर्थान् स्वाध्यायस्य विरोधिनः।
यथातथाध्यापयंस्तु साह्यस्य कृतकृत्यता।।
बुध्दिवृध्दिकराण्याशु धान्यानि च हितानि च।
नित्यं शास्त्राण्येवेक्षेत निगमांश्चैव वैदिकान्।।
— Manu IV, 17-19

2. वेदे षडङ्गे निरताः शुचयः सत्यवादिनः।
धर्मात्मानः कृतात्मानः स्युर्नृपाणां पुरोहिताः।।
— Adi, 159.17

प्रतिज्ञां चाधिरोहस्व कर्मणा मनसा गिरा।
पालयिष्याम्यहं भौमं ब्रह्म इत्यैव चासकृत्।।
यश्चात्र धर्मो नित्योक्तो दण्डनीतिव्यपाश्रयः।
तमशंकः करिष्यामि स्ववशो न कदाचन।।
अदण्डया मे द्विजाश्चेति प्रतिजानीहि हे प्रभो।
लोकं च संकरात्कृत्स्नं त्रातास्मीति परंतप।।
— Shanti 59, 106-108

3. ब्राह्मणं च पुरोधीत विद्याभिजनवाग्रूपवयः शीलसम्पन्नं
न्यायव्रतम् तपस्विनम्। तत्प्रसूतः कर्माणि कुर्वीत।
ब्रह्मप्रसूतं हि क्षत्रमृध्यते न व्यथत
इति च विज्ञायते।
—Gautam Smriti, Ch. XI

4. Shanti 84. 6-12.

5. धर्मेण च द्रव्यवृध्दौ आतिष्ठेद् यत्नभुत्तमम्।
दद्याच्च सर्वभूतानामन्नमेव प्रयत्नतः।।
compare,
दानमध्ययनं यज्ञः शौचेन धनसंचयः।
पितृवत्पालयेद्वैश्यो युक्तः सर्वपशूनिह।।
विकर्म तद्भवेदन्यत्कर्म यद्यत्समाचरेत्।
रक्षया स हि तेषां वै महत्सुखमाप्नुयात्।।
—Shanti 60, 21-22

6. *Bhartiya Samaj ka Aitihasik Vishleshan*, pp. 107-108.

7. In Mahabharata. (Sec XIII) there are a few episodes depicting extraordinary privileges allowed to guests, which include even intimate company of the wives of the host.

8. तस्य स्म शतमाचार्या वसन्ति सततं गृहे।
दर्शयन्तः पृथग्धर्मान्नानापाषण्डवादिनः।।
—Shanti 211.4

9. ततः परं कृतयुगे त्रेतायां ज्ञानमुत्तमम्।
द्वापरे यज्ञमाहुर्दानमेव कलौ युगे।।
—Shanti 224.27

10. Shanti 118. 10-18.

11. Sabha 49. 1-2.

12. Shanti 59. 105-106.

13. Shanti 16.5, 19.1.

14. *Ancient Indian Education*. 3rd Edition, p. 337.

3

Curriculum

Background

In the Vedic times our country had made a tremendous progress in various natural sciences. In those days sciences were divided mainly into two categories: Adhidaivika vidya and Adhyatma vidya. The sciences like Geology, Astronomy and Chemistry were called adhidaivika vidya. Similarly, Physiology, Psychology and Theology were called Adhyatma vidya. Of course, the works embodying the scientific knowledge of those times are entirely lost; but sufficient indications regarding various positive sciences are found in the Vedas, particularly in the Atharva veda.

The Mahabharata, being the epic of growth, cannot be attributed to one particular time. Form time to time, there had been profuse interpolations in the Epic by several scholars. It is opined by a group of scholars that this sort of interpolation continued till the Gupta period (5th century AD). However, the indications regarding various positive and natural sciences available in the Mahabharata reveal the extraordinary progress made in the field of sciences during the epic times.

Multi-dimensional Curriculum

From the data available in the Critical Edition (BORI, Pune) of the Mahabharata it is obvious that the ideas regarding curriculum had a very broad spectrum. It was not aimed only at spiritual growth but threads of worldliness are also visualized in the variety of the subjects taught at various centres of learning. It may be called multi-dimensional curriculum.

Traditional Lores

In the Kathopnishad lores are classified as Para (spiritual) and Apara (worldly). The former comprises four Vedas, six Vedangas, Upanishads,

Purana, Philosophy, Niti (morals), etc., whereas the latter encompasses History, Arthashastra, Astronomy, Astrology, Physics, Botany, Geology, Logic, Animal Husbandry, etc. Later on during the Buddhist period many useful arts and crafts were incorporated in the syllabus apart from the traditional religious literature. They can be classified as below :

1. *General Subjects*: Writing, arithmetic, geometry, arthashastra, etc.
2. *Arts and Crafts* : Weaving, spinning, dying, printing, music, iconography, painting, poetry, sculpture, etc.
3. *Vocational Subjects* : Farming, cattle-breeding, medical science (minor surgery, major surgery, medicine, personal and public hygiene, etc., 8 branches as mentioned in the treatises of Charak, Shushrut, etc.).
4. *Military Training* : Charioteering, club-fighting, archery, wrestling and other martial arts.

Before we come to the discussion on the above subjects, we would like to observe that in the Mahabharata we find the mention of these four traditional lores at different places in different contexts: Vedtrayee (three Vedas, *i.e.* Rik, Yajus and Sam), Anvikshiki (logic), Varta (farming, trade etc.) and Dandniti (statecraft).[1]

Different Viewpoints

It is worth mentioning here that the authorities differ as to the number of these traditional lores to be taught. Alike the Mahabharata, Kautilya (1.2) holds that these four sciences (lores) must be included in the royal education but his commentators' explanation of Anvikshiki differs from that of the Mahabharata. The commentators of Kautilya's *Arthashastra* have defined Anvikshiki as comprising Sankhya, Yoga and Lokayat (atheistic) philosophies. Regarding the rest three lores the Mahabharata and the Arthashastra opine identically.

The school of Manu (manava) held that philosophy was only a special branch of Vedic study and as such there were only three sciences (excluding Anvikshiki) to be studied. The school of Brahaspati held that there were only two sciences—Varta and Dandniti because "Vedic study" was "only an abridgement for a man experienced in temporal affairs". In other words, Brahaspati opined that a young prince or Kshatriya would not have the time to obtain more than a very casual acquaintance with the

Vedas. This view point seems to be more reasonable and appealing. The school of Ushnas (great exponent of Dandniti) declared that there was only one science, the science of Dandniti (science of government including a knowledge of criminal law), all others having their beginning in that. Although Kautilya admits four sciences as enumerated above, the first three are dependent on Dandniti; for Danda alone can procure safety and security of life which are very essential for any good State.

The above viewpoint regarding Dandniti is also found in the Mahabharata. As we have explained, it is an "Epic of growth", the growth of which was spread over the centuries. During such a long span of time, there were a lot of interpolations and manipulations and as such it is but natural to find therein a variety of viewpoints on many lores. These cannot and should not be taken as exceptions. But when we go into the details of the contexts of each viewpoint, we realise the broadmindedness of the subsequent writers, who put forth their viewpoint in proper contexts without refuting or undermining others' views, may it be on education, drinking, food habits or other aspects of human life.

Nature and Scope of Dandniti

Eulogizing Dandniti the Mahabharata says Rajdharma is the model for all types of conduct of the subjects. If Rajdharma (Dharma of Raja or conduct of the King) is not sound morally and spiritually, the conduct of the subjects cannot be correct, and the arts, crafts, literature (including Vedas) cannot prosper in the right direction. Rajdharma is said to be all-pervading, all-consuming and all-embracing.[2]

The Mahabharata advocates a "Welfare State" in the real sense of the term as is obvious from the questions posed by Narada in Sabha Parvan to the young king Yudhishthir: Does he support the widows and orphans of those who are perished for him in battle? Has he seen to a sufficiency of tanks, and seeds for sowing, and does he protect agriculture and trade and labour? Are taxes fair and ministers above bribery? Does he cherish, like a father, the blind, the lame, the dumb, the deformed, the friendless and homeless ascetics?

All these points were very pertinent and important which must be looked into by any ruler who claims to be the ruler of a Welfare State. Any amount of flow of funds and welfare measures cannot be effective if the officials and ministers indulge in malpractices and corruption. The ancient saying "as the king so the subjects" is always valid regardless of the place, time or form of government.

According to Manu (7.40-41) kings must be modest, for "many

kings have perished for lack of modesty", and thus Vena died and Nahusha fell and others likewise.

Danda rules all the people; Danda also protects; Danda wakens while they sleep; the sages say "Danda is Dharma" (Manu 7.17).

Dandniti was considered to be a very vast discipline and was indispensable for any young or old king. Dr. K.P. Jayaswal[3] has aptly said, "The treatises on political theories and practical governance were originally called 'Dand-Niti' or the 'Principles of Government' and Arthashastra or the 'code of commonwealth'. If at all we intend to define the nature and scope of Dandniti in modern terminology we can say that it comprises Economics, Political Science and Public Administration. Without having a sound and indepth knowledge not necessary insight into these subtle disciplines no ruler can rule in a befitting and just manner, may it be monarchy or democracy. Therefore, our ancient authorities laid great stress on 'Dandniti' as one of the subjects of the curriculum of that time.

In the Chhandogya Upnishad[4] we find the mention of all the subjects enumerated above. Before teaching the knowledge of "Self" to Narad, Sanatkumar desired to know the previous knowledge of Narada. Narada unfolded a long list of the texts over which he had acquired mastery. His inventory of these texts included the following: the four Vedas-Rig, Yajus, Sama and Atharva; the Epics and Puranas, the details of performance of the Shradha ceremony, grammar (Vyakarana), philology, mathematics, astronomy, magic, logic, philosophy; knowledge about the various gods of heaven and their powers, knowledge of animal life and knowledge of welfare. After reciting this long and impressive list, Narada, however, confessed to a feeling that, in spite of all that learning, he did not have the essence of knowledge. This episode reflects the significance of the knowledge of the self (Atma-Vidya or Adhyatma Vidya) during the upnishad period. This very feeling was well maintained and carried out in the epic period also.

Credibility of Learning

Regarding credibility of learning Kautilya held very frankly that these sciences should be learnt from the competent authorities otherwise they would not bear the desired fruit. He says, "Sciences shall be studied and their precepts strictly observed under the authority of specialist teachers. Having undergone the ceremony of tonsure, the students shall learn the alphabet and arithmetic. After investiture with sacred thread, he shall study the triple vedas, the science of Anvikshiki under teachers of acknowledged authority, the science of Varta under superintendents (heads of various departments as described in the Arthashastra), and the science of Dandniti under theoretical and practical politicians." It was emphasized that practical subjects should be learnt in close contact with their practice in actual life. In order to ensure credibility it was very essential.

The tragedy of the present system of education is that our examinations have lost their credibility totally because the T-L (Teaching-Learning) process suffers form lack of credibility. One of the prominent factors for this discredibility is the rapid erosion of our moral, academic, social and cultural values.

Footnotes

1. त्रयी चान्वीक्षिकी चैव वार्ता च भरतर्षभ।
   दण्डनीतिश्च, विपुला विद्यास्तत्र निदर्शिता।।
   — Shanti 59.33
   Compare, Arthashastra 1-2; Manu 7.43
2. सर्वे धर्मा राजधर्मप्रधानाः सर्वे धर्मा पाल्यमाना भवन्ति।
   सर्वत्यागो राजधर्मेषु राजंस्त्यागे चाहुर्धर्मग्र्यं पुराणम्।।
   मज्जेत् त्रयी दण्डनीतौ हतायां सर्वे धर्मा न भवेयुर्विरुध्दा।
   सर्वे धर्माश्चाश्रमाणां गता स्युः क्षात्रे व्यक्ते राजधर्मे पुराणे।।
   सर्वे त्यागा राजधर्मेषु दृष्टा सर्वा दीक्षा राजधर्मेषु चोक्ताः।
   सर्वे योगा राजधर्मेषु चोक्ताः सर्वे लोका राजधर्मान्प्रविष्टाः।।
   — Shanti 63.27-29
3. *Hindu Polity*, Bangalore (1967), p. 4.
4. *Chhandogya Upanishad*, 7/1/1-2.

4

Education—with Wide Spectrum

During the Mahabharata period education in the military science was at its peak. Throughout the country there were many schools (Ashramas) patronized by the State where an elaborate and intensive training in various military sciences was imparted. Situated at Hastinapur, Drona's Ashrama was one of them. Various characters of the epic received their education under the able guidance of Drona, Parsuram, Kripacharya and other Brahmin preceptors. The Brahmins no longer confined themselves strictly to the matters of religion and spiritual conduct but took keen interest in politics also. Brahmin warriors like Drona and Parsuram were counsellors to Kings not only in spiritual matters but also in warfare and several modalities of statecraft. In fact this age marked the growing rivalry between Brahmins and Kshatriyas. They started challenging the supremacy of each other. That is why we find a noble rishi in Janak, King of Mithila, and noblest warriors in Drona and Parsuram. However, the Brahmin class predominantly remained counsellors and rendered great services to the kings. Their contribution towards art, literature, philosophy, positive sciences, etc., cannot be overlooked. Similarly Kshatriyas (warrior class) enjoyed ultimate superiority in the use of weapons. Some law-givers such as Gautam (XI, 3) and Manu (vii, 43) enjoin that it is the King alone who is expected to commit to memory the Vedas, like the Brahmin, and not the ordinary members of his caste.

Contribution of Brahmins

The ashram of Jamdagni, son of Richeek, was also one of the famous centres for learning in the use of various weapons. Shardvat, son of the great sage Gautam, was a great exponent of archery. Even Lord Indra was scared of him.[1]

Shardwat and Jalpadi (1, 120, 6), a celestial girl, gave birth to Krip. Since he was brought up by the virtue of mercy (Kripa) of Shantanu (1,

120, 18), he was called Krip. Kripacharya, later on, became the preceptor of the Pandu, Vrishni and other princes (1, 120, 21).

Agniveshya, a prominent disciple of Agastya, was having his hermitage at Prayag. Dronacharya, son of Bhardwaj, and Drupad (father of Draupadi), had received their education (1, 121-9) at the hermitage of Agniveshya. Both of them were good friends in student life; but later on, when Drupad became King he refused to extend a helping hand to Drona in his rainy days, *i.e.* before getting appointed as the preceptor of the Pandu and Kuru princes. Drona felt insulted, and never forgot this. So, on the completion of education of the princes Drona insisted upon the defeat of Drupad by the princes as Guru-dakshina. Acharya Drona had received training in firearms (Agneyastra) from Agniveshya.[2]

Dronacharya had received intensive training in various arms from Bhargava Parsuram and studied Dhanurveda in depth.[3]

In the epic period the centres of military training (run with royal patronage) used to be quite sprawling. Cooks and other servants were there to look after the convenience of the trainees. Drona is found to have instructed the cook not to serve Arjuna in darkness.[4] Thus the preceptor used to keep a close watch on the routine of the trainees in order to keep them healthy and fit.

Competence in Warcraft

At the centres (hermitages) different skills of arranging or organizing the army were taught. Besides archery Drona had imparted the training Bhumi-yuddha (fighting on ground), Gaja-yuddha (fighting on elephant), Ratha-yuddha (fighting on chariot), club-fighting, etc. After the training was over diplomas were conferred according to one's competence in the attributive form such as Ardha-rathi, Rathi, Maharathi, Atirathi etc. Among the princes only Arjuna was declared as Atirathi.[5]

In Udyog parvan there is a sub-section (Up-parvan) called "Rathatirath-Sankhya" where the names of (warriors) Rathi, Maharathi, etc., have been enumerated on the first day of the war. In the Kaurava army Duryodhana and all his brothers are said to be the best Rathi, Whereas Kritverma, Shalya, Bhurishrava (son of Somdutt), Kripacharya, Dronacharya, etc., were Atirath. Karna has been described as "Ardharathi" only, which does not seem to be fair and just.

Training in Arms

Pandava princes were also expert in one lore or another. Though some of the scholars describe these princes as myths, they are now supposed to be real human figures. The eldest, Yudhishthira (the son of Dharma, virtue), is the Hindu ideal of excellence—just, calm, composed and compassionate, chivalrous, honourable and picture of cold heroism. As the name implies (firm in battle), he was of commanding stature and imposing presence. Bhima (meaning terrible) had mastered the use of club and was renowned for his gigantic size and giant strength.

The third, Arjuna, excelled all other princes in the skills of arms, and aroused the jealousy and hatred among the Kauravas. Drona had given him magical weapons. Both Bhima and Kuru Duryodhana had learnt the use of club from their cousin Balrama. When their education was completed, a tournament was held in which the youths displayed their skills in archery; in management of chariots, horses and elephants; in sword, spear and club exercises, and in wrestling. "Arjuna, after exhibiting prodigies of strength, shot five arrows simultaneously into the jaws of a revolving iron boar, and twentyone arrows into the hollow of a cow's horn, suspended by a string."

Bar of Low Descent

After Arjuna had completed his exhibition of various skills Karna appeared on the scene and did precisely the same deeds of skills, and challenged Arjuna to single combat; but as he could not tell his parentage nor he had any knighthood, he was not considered worthy to participate in the competition meant for royal youths.

Nakula, the fourth, learnt to tame horses and Sahdeva,[6] the fifth, became proficient in astronomy. Karna was not allowed to participate in the grand tournament since he was low-descended. Seeing such insult of Karna, Duryodhan uttered remarkable words:

> Noble deeds proclaim the warrior, and we
> question not their source!
> Teacher Drona, priest and warrior, own
> a poor and humble birth
> Kripa, noblest of Gautamas, springeth
> from the lowly earth,
> Know to me thy lineage Bhima, thine and thy
> borthers four,
> Amorous gods your birth imparted, so they say,
> in days of yore!

Mark the great and gallant Karna decked in
rings and weapons fair
She-deer breeds not lordly tiger in her
poor and lowly lair.[7]

From such instances we can not conclude that low descent was a bar to higher learning or the art of archery or any other super skill. Of course, examples like the refusal of Drona to Eklavya and of Parsuram to Karna are there in the Mahabharata. The former being the result of excessive love of Drona towards Arjuna and the latter of excessive hatred of Parsuram towards the warrior class (Kshatriyas) but these cannot be counted as a convention.

Thus we see that training in archery, sword-fighting, fist-fighting, club-fighting, riding, lifting and throwing of weights, driving of chariots had been some of the skills in which the warriors were supposed to be trained.

Stress on Physical Fitness

During the epic period the rulers, if they wanted to win the respect and esteem of the people, had to prove their valour and physical strength. The sacrifices like Rajasuya and Asvamedha were meant for such rulers only. We find quite an elaborate description of Rajasuya sacrifice in Sathpatha Brahmana. According to it there were three kinds of arrows: "Drava" (for mere shooting), "Ruja" (for piercing an enemy) and "Ksuma" (for missing the aim) were handed over to him who performed this sacrifice. Great significance was attached to physical capabilities of the ruler. The bow was truly a Kshatriya's strength. Another traditional sacrifice was "Vajapeya" Vajam meant strength and he who performed it was accepted as stronger than the others.

These three ceremonies cited above were associated with the coronation of kings and stressed upon physical fitness. Apart from these martial arts adequate training used to be imparted in statecraft and Vedic literature and several other lores useful and significant for a ruler.

The art of warfare consisted of various arts connected with the four-fold traditional divisions of the Indian army, *i.e.* the horse, the foot, the elephant and the chariot. All the arts and skills, tools and techniques of the age were comprehended by the generic term Dhanurveda (veda of the bow). In the Mahabharata various terms are found as attributives which connote various technicalities of warfare.

A few of them are as follows:

Shikshabalopet (शिक्षाबलोपेत)[8] – Equipped with the strength born of the skill acquired

Panilaghav (पाणिलाघव)[9] – Lightness of hand

Shashtr-grahan Vidya (शस्त्रग्रहणविद्या)[10] – Lightness of cleverness

Aaroh (आरोह) – Knowledge of seizing weapons

Paryavskand (पर्यावस्कन्द)[11] – Mounting a car

– Leaping down

Various Occupations and Vocations

In the Mahabharata there is a mention of various crafts, "Shilpaṃ Yashchopjivati".[12] In the Ramayana, Ram has been said as well-versed in various crafts of practical use—"Vaharikanam Shilpanam."[13] This term is, of course, indicative of various fine arts like music, painting, etc. In the Mahabharata[14] maid-servants of Yudhishthir have been described as very skilled in sixtyfour arts (which include various crafts also). These sixtyfour arts (Kalas) are well explained in Vatsyayana's Kamasutra.[15] The list of these sixtyfour arts is being illustrated as available in "Śukranitisara" in a more elaborate form. These sixtyfour kalas are found in many other works also including Kadambari, the Jain work Samavāyasutra, the Buddhist work Lalitvistara, Sutralankar of Asvaghosha, etc.

Sixtyfour Kalas

As far as the number of these kalas is concerned we find very interesting material in various Puranas and Smriti literature. The list of the sixtyfour kalas comprises the following :

1. Nartanam (dancing) accompanied by suitable and allied expressions through features of the face, movements of the arms and hands, and the like (havabhavadisamyukta).
2. Proficiency at playing on many instruments together in a concert, skills in playing an orchestra (aneka-vadyavikritau tadvadane jnanam).

   Vatsyayana mentions "Vina, Damaru and the like".

3. Skill at toilette, "assisting men and women in decorating themselves with dress and ornaments" (Stripurush vastralamkarasandhanam).
4. Anekarupavirbhava-kriti-jnanam, the art of producing various forms or figures out of stone, wood and other materials, the art of the sculptor.
5. Sayyastarana-samyoga-pushpadigrathanam, "the art of making beds and garlands with flowers".
6. Dyutadi-aneka-kridabhiranjnanam, "the art of entertaining by gambling, and other pastimes".
7. Anekasanasandhanairraterjnanam, the art of sporting with different postures.
8. Makarandasavadinam madyadinam kritih, "the art of preparing flower-juices and other intoxicating liquors".
9. Salyagudhahritau siravranavyadhe jnanam, "the art of extracting buried arrows, etc., and of incision of open wounds and blood-vessels".
10. Hinadirasasamyogannadisampachanam, the art of cooking various dishes with the various rasas combined in different proportions. Vatsyayana calls it "Vichitra-sakayusha-bhakshya-vikarakriya"—preparation of various vegetables, soups and condiments, and also "Panaka-rasa-raga-asava-yojanam"—the art of preparing different kinds of drinks.
11. Vrikshadi-prasava-aropa-palanadi kritih—the art of grafting and planting and culture of plants.
    Vatsyayana calls it Vrikshayurvedayogah—knowledge of the processes by which plants may be made to grow strong and healthy, abnormally small or big, etc.
12. Pashanadhatvadidritibhashmakaranam—the art of melting and reducing to ashes stones, minerals and the like.
    Vatsyayana calls it simply Dhatu-veda.
13. Yavadikshuvikarnam Kriti-jnanam—knowledge of the preparation of all things that can be prepared from the juice of sugarcane.
14. Dhatvaushadinam samyoga-kriya-jnanam—knowledge of the combination of minerals and herbs.
15. Dhatu-sankarya-parthakya-karanam—the art of combining and analyzing minerals.
16. Dhatvadinam samyoga-apurva-vijnanam—the science of producing new compounds of minerals.
17. Ksharanishkasana-jnanam—the art of extracting the Ksharas out of minerals.

18. Padadinyastah sastrasandhana nikshepah—art of adjusting the bow with the foot, fitting the arrow and then shooting it.
19. Sandhyaghta-krishtibhedaih mallayudham—the art of wrestling in different ways, utilizing grips and falls of diverse kinds.
20. Abhilakshite dese yantradi-astra-nipatanam—the art of hurling weapons and missiles at observed marks.
    The Kadambari mentions military proficiency in the art of wielding the different weapons of those days such as Chapa (bow and arrow), Chakra (discus), Varma (armour), Kripana (sword), Sakti (spear), Tomara (javelin), Parasu (axe), Gada (club), and the like.
21. Vadyasanketato vyuharachandi—the knowledge of forming an army into vyuhas in accordance with the directions conveyed by instrumental music.
22. Gajasvarathagatya tu yuddasamyojanam—taking part in battle on elephant, horse, or chariot.
23. Vividhasana-mudrabhih devata-toshanam—propitiating deities by worship in different postures and by different mudras or dispositions of fingers.
24. (Sarathyam—the sciences of charioteering.
25. Gajasvadeh gatisiksha—the art of training elephants and horses in movements.
26. Mrittika-kashtha-pashana-bhandadi-satkriya—the art of producing vessels and the like out of such material as clay, wood, stone or metals.
    Vatsyayana uses the following terms for some of these crafts: Pattika-Vetra-vana-vikalpah—making of different things like cots and seats from canes and reed.
27. Chitradi-alekhanam—painting of pictures.
    Vatsyayana calls it Alekhyam.
28. Tadaka-vapi-prasada-Samabhumi-Kriya—the art of digging tanks and wells and levelling the ground.
29. Ghattadi-anekayantranam vadyanam kritih—construction of machines like water-wheel and of musical instruments.
    Vatsyayana calls it yantramatrika which is explained as "construction of machines for purposes of locomotion, supply of water, and war".
30. Hina-madhyadi-samyga-varnadyai ranjanam—the art of painting with colours mixed in different proportions or quantities, large, moderate, and the like.
31. Jala-Vayu-Agni-Samyoga-nirodhaih kriya—working with water, fire, and air in two ways, by utilizing them or by controlling them.

32. Nauka-rathadir [illegible] anam kriti-jnanam—the science and art of constructing ships, chariots and other vehicles for locomotion.
33. Sutradi-rajjukarana-vijnanam—the art of making yarns, ropes, etc.
34. Anekatantu-samyogaih Patabandhan—weaving of cloth out of a variety of yarns.
35. Ratnanam vedhadisadasat jnanam—the science of testing precious stones, and of the processes of cutting and boring them and similar processes.
    Vatsyayana calls it Rupayaratna-pariksha—testing of precious stones and coins.
36. Svarnadinam yatharthya-vijnanam—the art of examining the properties of gold and testing its genuineness.
37. Kritrima-svarna-ratnadi-kriya-jnanam—the science and art of manufacturing artificial gold and imitation of precious stones.
38. Svarnadi-alamkara-kritih—manufacture of ornaments from materials like gold.
    Vatsyayana calls it Karna-patra-bhanga, which means the making of ear-ornaments.
39. Lepadi-satkritih—the art of enamelling, polishing varnishing, etc.
40. Charmanam mardavadi-kriya-Jnanam—the science and art of tanning leather.
41. Pasucharma-anga-nirhara-jnanam—the science of separating the hide and the various limbs from the bodies of animals.
42. Dugdhadohadi-ghritanam vijnanam—knowledge of the processes of milking and of making ghee from milk as its ultimate product.
43. Kanchukadinam sivane vijnanam—the art of sewing bodies.
    Vatsyayana use the general term Suchivana-karmanithe—art of sewing, weaving, knitting, and plaiting, by the use of needle.
44. Jale bahavadibhih taranam—the art of swimming in water with hands.
45. Griha-bhandadeh marjane vijnanam—the art of cleansing houses and household utensils and furniture.
46. Vastra-sammarjanam—the art of cleaning clothes, laundry.
47. Kshura-karma—the art of shaving.
48. Tila-mamsadi-snehanam nishkasane kritih—the art of extracting the essence out of sesamum, meats, and fats.
49. Sirady-karshane-jnanam—the art of ploughing, hoeing, etc.
50. Vrikshadi-arohane jnanam—the art of climbing trees and the like.
51. Manonukulasevayah kriti-jnanam—the art of serving another to his heart's content.

52. Venu-trinadi-patranam kriti-jnanam—the art of making vessels out of bamboo, reeds, etc.
53. Kacha-patradi-karana-vijnanam—the science of manufacturing vessels and other articles out of glass.
54. Jalanam samsechanam samharanam—the science of irrigation by which water is distributed and collected.
55. Lohadisar sastra-astra-kritijnanam—the art of manufacturing weapons out of metals.
56. Gaja-asva-vrishabha-ushtranam balyandi-kriya—the art of manufacture of saddles, etc., to be used for riding elephants, horses, bullocks and camels.
57. Sishoh samkarshane dharane kridane jnanam—the art of bringing up, handling, and playing with children.
58. Aparadhijaneshu yuktatadana-jnanam—the art of handling offenders by suitable rebukes.
59. Nanadesiya-varnanam susamyak lekhane jnanam—proficiency in writing the alphabets of various countries.
60. Tambularakshadi kriti-vijnanam—the art of preparing tambula, *i.e.* betel-nuts, arecanuts, slaked lime, etc.
61. Adanam—power of comprehension of these Kaḷas.
62. Asukaritvam—quickness of work.
63. Pratidanam—imparting instruction in the Kalas.
64. Chirkriya—slow or gradual work.

From the perusal of the above sixtyfour Kalas, it will be clear that the list includes not only arts but various crafts and vocations also. When the Mahabharata says that the maidservants of Yudhishthir were well-versed in sixtyfour Kalas, it simply means that they know the practical implications of many of these arts. In the poetical form of the version such exaggeration is but natural. The nomenclatures of these kalas show the diverse spectrum of occupations and vocations available during that age. It also gives us good account of the economic and cultural life prevailing during the epic period.

Medical Science

From the various references in the epic which include quick cure of injured soldiers, calling of surgeons and physicians by "Duryodhana for the treatment of Bhishma, advice of Narad to Yudhishthir for giving proper facilities to the physicians, etc., it is obvious that medical science had made good progress during the epic period.

Sir William Hunter has rightly remarked about ancient Hindu medicine and surgery. He observes: "Indian medicine dealt with the whole area of the science. It described the structure of the body, its organs, ligaments, muscles, vessels, and tissues. The Materia Medica of the Hindu embraces a vast collection of drugs belonging to the mineral, vegetable and animal kingdoms, many of which have been now adopted by European physicians."

As regards surgery, he writes: "They conducted amputations practised lithotomy; performed operations on the abdomen and uterus; cured hernia, fistula, piles; set broken bones and dislocations, and were dexterous in the extraction of foreign substances from the body. A special branch of surgery was devoted to rhinoplasty, or operation for improving deformed ears and noses and forming new ones.... They were expert in midwifery, not shrinking from the most critical operations, and in the diseases of women and children."

Sushruta describes not less than one hundred and twenty surgical instruments and a large number of surgical operations. It has been rightly observed by Sushruta that "no accurate account of any part of the body, including even the skin, can be rendered without a knowledge of anatomy; hence, anyone who wished to acquire a thorough knowledge of anatomy must prepare a dead body and carefully examine all its parts."

During the epic period medical science registered very good progress in the fields of minor and major surgery, midwifery, toxicology, etc. There are eight branches of medical science and as such the science was popularly called "Ashtanga Ayurveda". In Sabha Parvan, Narad poses a question to Yudhishthir, "Whether the physicians skilled in all the eight branches of Ayurveda attend to your health or not?".[16] In the Mahabharata we come across the names of several acharyas, who contributed substantially to the development of Ayurveda, which include Jatukaran, Parasar, Gautam, Kamkayan, Gargya Galava, Satyaki, Shaunak, Kashyap, Ushna (Shukracharya), Nakul, etc. Although their treatises are not available, their opinions are found scattered in various commentaries of famous treatises on Ayurveda.

Medical profession was considered to be one of the noble professions. It had its own code of ethics which is elaborated in the treatise of Charaka who was the best physician of his time. According to him "not for money, nor for any earthly object, should one treat his patients; in this way the physician's work excels all other vocations. Those who sell treatment, as an article of trade, neglect the true treasure of gold in search of mere dust."

These admonitions were followed sincerely by the physicians of the epic time.

Veterinary Science

Pandava Nakul was a great exponent of the horse lore (Ashwa-vidya), whose treatise on cattle-breeding, etc., named "Ashwachikitsa" is available these days. His twin-brother Sahdev was also an expert in animal-husbandry. He had the skill to diagnose the disease on the basis of the urine of a sick bull. Both of these had learnt these lores from Dronacharya.

Nakul was such an expert in the horse lore that he could diagnose the disease by first examining the colour of the urine of a horse.

Similarly monographs on the element lore are also available. All these instances reveal that considerable advances were made in the veterinary science.

Botany

Sir J.C. Bose, a famous botanist, earned world wide fame for his famous theory called "Pulsation Theory of Ascent of Sap in Plant Life. This theory was later challenged by many other scientists including Godvesky who propounded a theory of vital forces. On this theme, a recent book is "The Secret of Plants" by Peter Tompkins and Christopher Bird. Its sub-title reads: *Astounding discoveries about the physical, emotional and spiritual relations between plants and man.* It is a fascinating account of the researches on the subject conducted in the United States, Soviet Russia and other countries. In the "Introduction" to their book the authors have rightly observed:

"Evidence now supports the vision of the poet and philosopher that plants are living, breathing, communicating creatures, endowed with personality and attributes of soul. It is only we, in our blindness, who have insisted on considering them automata."

The Mahabharata is replete with such evidence to prove that plants and trees do have sense organs and soul. In Book XII (Shanti parvan, Ch. 177) the question has been posed whether trees have life. It is answered in the affirmative and emphatically, explaining the various actions of plants like seeing, hearing, eating, breathing, etc., with proper reasoning. Thus it has been firmly established that plants have life.[17] How astonishing a similarity between the vision of Vyas and the conclusion of modern scientists.

The Indian vision of the spiritual unity in all existence, man and tree alike, is reflected in our Vedas also. The Rigved confirms this unity and propounds that plants have lives. In one of the hymns of the Rigved[18] it is said that the God of Wind (Maruta) with his thunder makes even the mountains to shiver, the trees and plants also get stumbled just as a woman sitting in a chariot gets stumbled due to the movements of the chariot. Here it is clearly mentioned that trees shiver due to fear. But in the Mahabharata we find quite an elaborate description of various live activities of trees with specific reasoning behind their each action like seeing, hearing, moving, enjoying, sorrowing, etc.[19]

The authors of "The Secret Life of Plants" have rightly concluded their book with these words:

> "The attraction of the seer's supersensible world, or worlds within worlds, is too great to forego, and the stakes are too high, for they may include survival for the planet. Where the modern scientist is baffled by the secrets of the life of plants, the seer offers solutions which, however incredible, make more sense than the dusty mouthings of academicians; what is more, they give philosophic meaning to the totality of life."

Footnotes

1. धनुर्वेदपरत्वाच्च तपसा विपुलेन च।
   भृशं संतापयामास देवराजं गौतमः।।
   —Adi 120.5
2. Adi 121. 6-7.
3. Adi 121.22.
4. Adi 123.2.
5. Adi 123.43.
6. Even nowadays a man well-versed in astronomy is called Sahdev in some parts of Maharashtra and Chhattisgarh.
7. R.C. Dutta, *The Mahabharata condensed into verse*, p. 12.
8. 7.45.17.
9. 6.74.10.
10. 6.76.7.
11. 6.76.8.
12. Anu 90.8.
13. Ramayan 2.1.28.
14. चतुष्षष्ठिविशारदाः, Sabha 61.9.
15. *Kamasutra*, Section I, Chapter III.
16. कच्चिद्वैद्याश्चिकित्सायामष्टाङ्गायां विशारदाः।
    सुहृदाश्चानुरक्ताश्च शरीरे ते हिते रताः।। Sabha 5.8

A similar question was posed by Ram to Bharat at Chitrakoot.

"कच्चित्............वैद्यान्........चाभिमन्यसे।"

Ramayana 2.100-113

17. ग्रहणात् सुखदुःखस्य छिन्नस्य च विरोहणात्।
जीवं पश्चामि वृक्षानामचैतन्यं न विद्यते।।

—Shanti 177.17

18. यत्त्वेष यामा नर्दयत पर्वतान्दिवो वा पृष्टं नर्या अचुच्यवुः।
विश्वो वो अज्मन्भयते वनस्पति रथयन्तीव प्रजिहीत ओषधिः।।

19. Shanti 177. 11-13.

5

System of Values

Inculcation of values is one of the significant aims of any literature. In one way or the other each work, may it be an epic or Upnishad or a drama of the great poet Kalidasa, conveys some message. In the Kavya Prakash of Mammat three modes have been described for conveying such a message or putting forth a piece of advice to its readers, *i.e.* master-like, friend-like and a sweet lady-like (kantasammit). Shastras like the Vedas, Upnishads, etc., adopt the first mode whereas kavya (poetry) adopts the other two modes for advising its readers. Since the Shastras the first kind of works—neither present ideals nor examples before their readers they do not have any scope to introduce the stories. But just the opposite is the case of the kavyas. They have ample scope for introducing stories to give examples or to present ideals before their readers.

Total Concern for Values

The Mahabharata certainly belongs to the second category of the works mentioned above. It propounds "primarily spiritualistic and yet realistic, humanistic and individualistic and yet socialistic and universalistic, ancient and yet dynamic and progressive" system of values. Depiction of such a value system has been done in the epic through a large number of stories. It is not the essential quality of all the epics as we do not find such stories in the great epic like the Ramayana. It is peculiar to the Mahabharata only because of its peculiar nature and the sublime and subtle aim of its author(s). According to Dr. A. Sengupta "the social outlook in the Mahabharata is essentially humanitarian as the social ideal is to awaken in man all human excellences which will make him fit for the realisation of his own infinity and bliss. It is only when a man attains moral qualities that his mind is elevated to a higher level, and in that elevated state of consciousness is realised the infinite being of an embodied soul".

The fact is that the Mahabharata is not simply an epic or a literary composition. Anyone who reads this great epic will be convinced of the fact that it is not simply a specimen of poetic art; but rather a treatise on philosophy, religion, ethics, politics, morality, a law-book and a historical record as well; and consequently the different kinds of stories find scope to be introduced to explain and illustrate the maxims related to these treatises.

The nature of the plot of this great epic also adds to its capacity to allow scope to introduce stories. It is not possible to introduce stories in all epics because their plots are such that there is no occasion to say different kinds of things. But the plot of the Mahabharata is such that all kinds of subjects can be introduced or absorbed in it. The plot of this epic is a political feud between the cousins of a royal family. It will be easily admitted that politics is such a subject which can absorb all kinds of thoughts in it. It is this nature of the epic which has made it possible to successfully introduce different kinds of subjects, and hence different kinds of stories, to explain the well-defined maxims related to them.

Now the question may arise as to why the author of this great epic selected such a plot and why he introduced so many subjects in it. To answer this question one may turn to Dr. V.S. Sukathankar, in whose opinion this mighty work is primarily concerned with finding a solution to the problem of evil in life, nay, to the problem of existence itself. We may add that the aim of the author of the Mahabharata is not only to deal with the problems of human existence but also to find out the way of achieving the four-fold aim of human life, *i.e.* Artha, Kama, Dharma, and Moksha. It is this aim of the author of the epic which has directed him to select such a plot for his epic and to introduce all kinds of subjects which, directly or indirectly, are related to this aim. And whatever ideas or instructions he found fit to be taught to the people, he tried to achieve his aim through the medium of stories.

Dharma : A Central Value

Prof. Prativa Verma[1] has rightly remarked, "The Mahabharata lays great stress on the values of Dharma, Artha and Kama which help the realisation of Moksha, *i.e.* the complete welfare of the individual and the community. The universe is ever-changing. Objects of diverse characters are trying to evolve, transform and accomplish themselves. Man, too, is constantly exerting to fulfil himself, to surpass his finitude and to become infinite, deathless and divine. Moksa is, therefore, the supreme value for a man. Moksa means overcoming all limitations and realizing man's inherent or true universality, truth, beauty and goodness".

The great epic remarks that both death and deathlessness are rooted in man. Ignorance leads him to death and finitude while knowledge enables the realization of deathlessness, the supreme value. As a result of ignorance, a man forgets his true nature, identifies himself with his body, mind, senses, etc., or all that is perishable, tries to satisfy his superficial and perishable nature and suffers miseries. The true man is really eternal, infinite, subtle and universal. He is the ground of all the manifestations, the eternal light and consciousness underlying all objects. He is Truth and Immortality. Man's body, senses, mind, life-breath, blood, flesh and bones—all these are subject to death and decay. It is only the spirit within which undergoes no change. But this spirit, the eternal light within, is too subtle to be grasped easily. Therefore, the Mahabharata asks a man to exert constantly to grasp it with the help of wisdom. A wise and industrious man, who exerts with strong determination, never fails to realize the supreme value, the summum bonum.

Multi-dimensional Approach

Since the author of the Mahabharata wanted to spread his ideas, especially those regarding Dharma, even to the man in the street, he chose the medium of stories. Story, in fact, is the best medium because even the busiest man finds some time to hear stories for his recreation and learn, unconsciously, something very useful for his life. "No decalogue," it is well said, "has half the influence on human conduct that is exercised by a single drama or page of narrative". The author of the epic knew fully the fact that the story-telling method would be the fittest to prepare the man in the street to grasp and follow his advice.

Here one may ask why, at all, the author of the Mahabharata has attempted to spread his ideas and good advice to each and every one? What was the need of spreading these instructions even to the man in the street who was not inclined to learn anything? The reason is obvious. As has been mentioned above, the author was busy finding a solution to the problem of human existence on earth and also to the problem of finding out the ways of achieving the four-fold aim of human life. And this aim would not be achieved unless and until each and every human being was taken into confidence. Whether a human being is learned or not, is roaming in the street or sitting on the throne, he is still a human being, and a single human being is enough to destroy or build a whole society. Hence for the real happiness of mankind it is necessary, nay, essential to reform each and every human being on earth. Therefore, the author of the epic is clearly eager to acquaint even the man in the street with his good advice. Since he wanted to reform and elevate all men, he has offered his instructions in a friendly manner, generally through the medium of stories. In the words of V.S. Sukthankar, "The vast canvass of this gigantic epic is studied with little instructive episodes dealing with all manner of relations and situations in life, which the epic tries to study by putting them under the microscope and illuminating them from its own point of view. We find there stories throwing light on the relations between a king and his subjects, between a master and his servants, between parents and children, between husband and wife, between man and man and, above all, between man and God. The situations depicted are equally varied and numerous. As Sister Nivedita has so lucidly and incisively put it, "the stories embody the endeavour on the part of the epic poets to understand every man's relation to a given situation and to see in conflicting lines of conduct that same irresistible necessity which, acting from within, hurls each one of us upon its fate." We observe this in the life and fate of Bhishma and Dhritrashtra, of Duryodhana and Vidura, of Kunti and Karna, of Yudhishthira and Arjuna.

Now it is to be seen how the author of the epic has taken help of different kinds of stories to impart instruction. It will not be out of place here to mention that though the attainment of Artha, Kama, Dharma and Moksha cannot be said to be quite independent of the problem of human existence, yet it has been so treated here only for the sake of convenience.

Whatever instruction or advice the author thought fit for the achievement of his aim, to emphasise that point he either invented a story or drew upon the sources available to him. For example, the first thing that is absolutely necessary for the existence of the human race on this earth is the building up of a good society. A good society means a group of good people. Therefore, the author has tried his best to make each individual a good constituent of society. Since a society cannot prosper unless it is properly arranged and managed, he advises the people to follow the varnashramadharma and to explain and illustrate it he has introduced stories.

Kingdom and King

The author was fully acquainted with the fact that for maintaining peace in society and for its management a king or a head of governmental machinery was necessary. Hence he has described the necessity of a king in the form of a story. Yudhishthira asks Bhishma to explain how the king came into existence, who being equal in all respects to an ordinary man, protects the earth and who is so important for the people that the whole region becomes happy or unhappy after him. Then Bhishma tells him that previously there was neither a kingdom nor a king, neither danda nor dandika. When all the people, subjugated by greed and desire, destroyed their knowledge and Dharma and when the veda and the Dharma perished, the gods were afraid and they went to Brahman and asked him to do good for them.

When requested like this, Brahman composed the Nitisastra, containing one lakh chapters, on Artha, Kama and Dharma. This treatise was abridged by Sankara, Indra, Brihaspati and lastly by Sukracharya in one thousand chapters. After that the gods went to Vishnu and on their request he created a man named Virajas by the power of his mind. But this mind-born son of Vishnu did not want to become a king. The fourth descendant of this Virajas and the son of Kardama, viz. Ananga, became the first king who was the protector of the people and was expert in Dandaniti. Telling this story[2] Bhishma explained the word *rajan* which meant one who makes the people happy. From this story it is clear that for the protection of the people and for peace in society a king is absolutely required. Since the king is so important, and since the happiness and unhappiness of the people depend on him, he himself must be good. And to make the king good and efficient the author of the epic has discussed the duties of a king. This is the reason why the following subjects were considered by the author of the Mahabharata as of special importance : (i) the duties of a king, the king being the recognized head of the government machinery which regulates the socio-political structures; and (ii) conduct in times of calamity, applicable to (king and Brahmana) the first two varnas of the Indian society, when the ordinary codes of conduct are not applicable. It is clear that the author did not want the king to be free to do what he liked but wanted to make him do what really might be ideal for the society.

Thus we see that "Each One Teach One" (oftly quoted slogan in Adult Education) appears to be the motto of the poet in narrating various episodes indicative of different ethical, social and spiritual values. While introducing such episodes he invariably says "here (in this context) also such ancient historical episode has been narrated".[3]

Secularity in Outlook

Dr. A.S. Altekar opines that "the State was to promote Dharma, not by championing any particular sect or religion, but by fostering a feeling of piety and religiousness, by encouraging virtue and morality, by extending help to establishments belonging to all religions and sects, by maintaining free hospitals and feeding houses for the poor and the decrepits and, last but not least, by extending patronage to literature and sciences"[4] All these acts have been incorporated in the daily routine of the king in Kautilya's Arthashastra. The then priests were supposed to observe whether the king performs his duties and exercises his authority as per the norms or not though not very meticulously at times. The epic enjoins the king to look after the wellbeing of the orphans, old people, widows, etc., invariably.[5]

On the part of the individual also it was rather obligatory to lead his/her life according to his/her Dharma. In fact it was the coercive authority of the State which created an automatic tendency to follow one's Dharma. The divinity of the king was also regarded as justifying the political obligations of the citizen.

Divinity of King Questioned

Though Manu[6] and other writers have confirmed the theory of "King's Divinity," during later times it was not abided by. As we have already mentioned the Mahabharata is an epic of growth and as such the value system as visualized in the epic is very complex and at times rather self-contradictory. On the one hand it says that the King deserves all divine dignity[7], as it has been narrated in the "Divine Theory" of Hobbes (19th century), on the other, it does not impose on citizens an absolute obligation to bow to his authority. The epic clearly mentions that the king's divinity should be honoured only till such time as he does not deviate from the path of Dharma, or he manifests his divine qualities in the larger interest of his subjects and looks after their welfare in an appropriate manner. This appropriately does not consist at all in the championship of varna and ashramas, which led to many misunderstandings and ultimately iniquitous social order. It has been aptly remarked that varnadharma or the caste system in particular is based upon iniquitous principles; it exalts the Brahmana and confers almost divine honours upon him, while it reduces the Shudras and Chandalas almost to the position of slaves, denying them the most elementary rights of ordinary citizenship. The Shudras were prevented from holding property and were subjected to more heavier punishments for identical offenses. The Chandalas were treated worse than dogs. Actually such iniquitous acts have maligned the image of the social orders of the Hindus. Here just it can be mentioned that the State only enforced what had been previously approved or disapproved by social conscience. In the ancient literature on polity we do not come across any legislative enactment by any king for such inhuman and heinous acts.

Coming to the topic we can say that the king was, no doubt, divine but the laws and customs were still more so and the king had no authority to change them suiting to this own convenience or interest. If the king deviated from these laws and customs, turned tyrant neglecting the well being of his subjects and become guilty of gross misbehaviour and misgovernment the citizens were permitted to depose and even execute the king.[8] The king was required to take a vow at his coronation that he would scrupulously protect and respect them. In the case of a breach of the vow on his part the subjects were permitted to execute the king. The Mahabharata expressly recognizes the subjects' right to tyrannicide if there was no other remedy left to them.[9]

Spiritualism vs. Materialism

Artha has been regarded as a great social value in the epic. Being instrument to the individual and social prosperity and material happiness it can be termed as an instrumental value. Here we may recall the version of Yajnyavalkya, a great champion of spiritual science, who says that "the wealth is not dear to one simply because it is wealth; but it is dear to one because it is dear to one's oneself.[10] In one's life wealth (Vitta) helps one in attaining other values like charity, hospitality, sacrifice, happiness, kindness, satisfaction of desires, etc. Therefore, the Mahabharata recommends Artha as a normal object of human pursuit. But simultaneously warns that wealth should not be treated as of an intrinsic value. It must be pursued only as an instrument to realize Dharma and Kama. It has been rightly said that wealth helps the wise and governs the foolish.

Though among the trinity of social values (Dharma, Artha and Kama) Dharma has been recognized as the most important value, due importance has also been given to Artha. Just before the beginning of the great war Yudhisthir approached his elderly preceptors like Bhishma, Dronacharya and Kripacharya to seek their blessings in their respective tents. Their hearts were overwhelmed by agony and repentance (being on the side of Duryodhana knowingly). Bhishma so confessed and said that because of Duryodhana's great obligation on him he was fighting for Duryodhana in spite of the proven fact that he was on the unrighteous path. Further he says, "A man is a slave to the wealth, while wealth is not a slave to anyone. This is a truth. That is why O King Yudhishthir, I am duty-bound towards the Kauravas.[11] The same version was repeated by Dronacharya and Kripacharya also. This is indicative of the correct though painful approach to values then. Due to indigent conditions when Dronacharya approached King Drupad (father of Draupadi) for monetary help Drupad had refused to recognize him as a friend, though they had studied together for years at the ashram of Bhardwaj, father of Drona.[12] Drupad's father's name was Prishat. Bhardwaj and King Prishat were close friends.[13] That is why Prishat had sent his son Drupad for studies to Bhardwaj. Thus Drona and Drupad were also close friends. But after becoming the King of Panchal he refused to recognize the old friendship saying, "A poor man (Araja) cannot be a friend of a King (Raja)." Being very annoyed and disgusted Drona approached the court of the Pandavas and was appointed by Bhishma as a tutor of the princes (Kauravas and Pandavas). After having trained the princes to wage a war against Drupad. Consequently there was a great war in which, Bhim and Arjuna defeated king Drupad. After his wish was fulfilled Drona not only forgave Drupad but also returned half of his Kingdom (Panchal). Having accepted the lot Drupad shifted his capital from Ahichhatrapur to Kampilya[14]. Draupadi's Swayamvar (selection of bridegroom by the bride herself) was held at Kampilya only.

Thus materialistic trends prevailing in the then social structure have clearly been visualized by Vyas in the epic. At one place he says that the sum total of our all efforts and endeavours is just for a handful of rice. "Sarvarambhah Tandulprithmoolah".

Further he observes that the very structure of society is based on trade and commerce, which always keep it in proper function. Trade and commerce flourish when there is proper government.[15] Let us examine the very term 'Varta' which stands for trade and commerce. 'Varta' was one of the four prominent lores mentioned in the epic. These are: Triyee (study of three Vedas), Anvikshiki (logical science—Nyaya), Varta (trade and commerce) and Dandniti (political science and state craft).[16] In the epic mainly three professions were there—agriculture, cattle-breeding and commerce—mainly attributed to the business class (Vaishyas)[17]. It has been clearly mentioned that if a Vaishya (businessman) wants to derive happiness in life he should breed the cattle with great care and caution, just like he would serve his parents. On his part all other functions are not to be said as good.[18] It is also worth-noticing here that while underlining the significance of the epic, it has been described as Artha-shastra, Dharma-shastra and Moksha-shastra and thus the first place is given to Arthashastra.[19]

In the Mahabharata great importance has been attached to friendship as a value of life. It is said that the company of good men and good friends is superior to that of even blood relations. Proverbially it is said that a man is known by the company he keeps. Company of fools and ignorant people brings misfortune while that of good, learned and virtuous men brings prosperity. Therefore, it is advised that one should always seek the company of and friendship with only the learned and virtuous persons. It was opined and is time-tested now that a wise enemy is better than a foolish friend.

In the epic, Duryodhana represents lust for property and Kichak lust for pleasure, in total neglect of the ethical values. They hanker after property and pleasure respectively regardless of the morals of the day which leads to their ignoble and miserable end. This enjoins that Kama or Artha should not be pursued as intrinsic values. If they are pursued for their own sake they lead an individual to various evils.

Karma vs. Destiny

The Mahabharata described Karma as an important value. One's own Karma is the instrument to his fortune or misfortune. The wise depend upon their own industry and endeavour and not merely on their destiny. Karma has rightly said:

सूतो वा सूतपुत्रो वा यो वा को वा भवाम्यहम्।
दैवायत्तं कुले जन्म मदायत्तं तु पौरूषम्।।

> may be a charioteer (Soot) or son of a charioteer (Sootputra), whatever I may be, it depends upon God; but valour and gallantry are my own.

There had been a difference of opinion on the point whether an individual's fortune or misfortune depends upon his destiny or on his own effort and industry, as it prevails in modern times also. In the Mahabharata even after an expression of a balanced view, more importance has been given to Karman only as the following verse indicates:

यथा ह्येकेन चक्रेण रथस्य गतिर्न विद्यते।
तथा पुरुषकारेण विना दैवं न सिध्यति।।

As the chariot cannot move with a single wheel, so is the case with an individual's destiny. Without sustained efforts destiny cannot be fulfilled.

Positive and Negative Values

In the Mahabharâta positive and negative human values have been termed as divine and demoniacal respectively. The Bhagavadgeeta, a part of the epic (Bhishma Ch. 23-40 in the Critical Edition), describes these qualities as follows:

Positive or Divine Values

Fearlessness, absolute purity of heart, constant absorption of mind in meditation for self-realization and the sattvic form of charity, control of senses, worship (of God as well as celestial beings and superiors) and the performance of Agnihotra (pouring oblations into the sacred fire) and other auspicious acts, study of the Vedas and other sacred texts, chanting of divine names and glories, bearing of hardships for the sake of one's own Dharma and straightness of mind, including straightness of the body and senses.

Non-violence in thought, word and deed, truthfulness and geniality of speech, absence of anger even on provocation, renunciation of the idea of doership in action, tranquillity of mind, refraining from malicious gossip, kindness to all creatures, absence of attachment to the objects of senses even during their contact with the senses, mildness, sense of shame in doing things not sanctioned by the scriptures or usage, abstaining from idle pursuits.

Sublimity, forgiveness, fortitude, external purity, absence of malice, absence of the feeling of self-importance these are the marks of the one who is naturally endowed with divine virtues, O descendant of Bharata.[20]

Negative or Demoniacal Values

Divine values are regarded as conducive to liberation, whereas negative or demoniacal values are supposed to be conducive to bondage. In the Gita,[21] hypocrisy, arrogance, pride, anger, harshness and ignorance these are mentioned as demoniacal values. Men cherishing such type of values are not able to distinguish between good and bad. They do not know what is right activity and what is right cessation of activity. Therefore, they possess neither purity (internal or external) nor good conduct nor truth.

Possessed of hypocrisy, conceit and given to insatiable passion, and adopting false doctrines due to delusion, they take to action with impure vows. Giving themselves over to endless cares terminating only in death, and given to the enjoyment of sensuous pleasures, they believe the highest limit of joy to consist only in this. Held in bondage by a hundred ties of expectation, given over to passion and anger, they strive to obtain by unlawful means hoards of money for the enjoyment of sensuous pleasure.[22]

At one place Yudhishthir asks Bhishma about the symptoms of the good and the wicked persons. On this the reply endorsed by Bhishma is apparently indicative of the positive and negative values. Bhishma says that "the wicked are ungovernable and foul-mouthed". What the virtues do on the other hand is regarded as the clue to the course of conduct which is called good. But the virtuous stand aside and give the way to the old, those carrying heavy burdens, women, those in authority in the village or town administration, Brahamanas, and the Kings. Good conduct is the root of all prosperity, fame and longevity. Indeed it is said to be superior to all branches of knowledge. Thus Bhishma has stressed upon the truly practical, that is, good conduct. He further states that the bliss which is the fruit of righteousness is not eternal as it is destined to come to an end in certain cases.

However, righteousness is eternal. Righteousness alone is one's friend as per the advice of Bhishma. Thus the message of the Mahabharata is the message of truth and righteousness. According to the epic, in sum, righteousness is the way which has been followed and lived, with perfect purity of heart, by the wise and the learned, who have neither likes nor dislikes, who wish well of all creatures, who are knowers of the Vedas and whose conduct conforms to the standard of Dharma. The followers of righteousness attain the highest good, though this dictum may appear to be ironical keeping in view the current phenomena of a high degree of degeneration in our moral, ethical and social values.

Footnotes

1. Prof. Prativa Verma, *Social Philosophy in Mahabharata and Manu Smriti*, p.130.
2. नैव राज्यं न राजासीन्न दण्डो न दण्डिकः।
   धर्मेणैव प्रजाः सर्वा रक्षन्ति च परस्परम्।।
   पाल्यमानास्तथान्योन्यं नरा धर्मेण भारत।
   खेदं परमाजग्मुस्ततस्तान्मोह आविशत्।।
   ते मोहवशमापन्ना मानवा मनुजर्षभ।
   प्रतिपत्तिविमोहाच्च धर्मस्तेषाभनीनशत्।।

नष्टायां प्रपिपत्तौ तु मोहवश्या नरास्तदा।
लोभस्य वशमापन्नाः सर्वे भारतसत्तम।।

— Shanti 59.14-17

3. अत्राप्युदाहरन्तीममितिहासं पुरातनम्।
4. Dr. A.S. Altekar. *State and Government in Ancient India*, p.48.
5. Mahabharata, Shanti 86.24.
6. बालोऽपि नावमन्तव्यो मनुष्यो इति भूमिपः।
महती देवता हयेषा नररुपेण तिष्ठति।।

— Manu VII.8

7. मानुषाणामधिपतिं देवभूतं सनातनम्।
देवाश्च बहु मन्यन्ते धर्मकामं महेश्वरम्।।

— Shanti 65.29

न जातु अवमन्तव्यो मनुष्य इति भूमिपः।
महती देवता हयेषा नररुपेण तिष्ठति।।

8. अरक्षितारं हर्तारं विलोप्तारामदायकम्।
तं स्म राजकलिं हन्युः प्रजाः संभूय निर्घणम्।।

— Anu 60.19

9. अहं वो रक्षितेत्युक्त्वा यो न रक्षति भूमिपः।
स संहत्य निहंतव्यः श्वेव सोन्माद आतुरः।।
Shukraniti (IV.I.3) recommends that they should first warn the tyrant king that they would migrate from the country and go to another, which was better governed. Perhaps it was hoped that the prospective loss of revenue may bring the king to his senses.
10. न वा अरे वित्तस्य काभाय वित्तं प्रियं भवति।
आत्मनस्तु कामाय वित्तं प्रियं भवति।।

— Chhandogya Upanishad

11. अर्थस्य पुरुषो दासो दासस्त्वर्थो न कस्यचित्।
इति सत्यं महाराज बध्दोऽस्म्यर्थेन कौरवैः।।

— Bhishma 41.36

12. स नित्यमाश्रमङ्गत्वा द्रोणेन सह पार्षतः।
चिक्रीडाध्ययनं चैव चकार क्षत्रियर्षभ।।

— Adi 111.18

13. भरद्वाजसरवा चासीत् पृषतो : नाम पार्थिव।

— Adi 111.16

14. Adi Parvan, Ch.140
15. वार्तामूलो हयं लोकस्तथा वै धार्यते सदा।
तत्सर्वं वर्तते सम्यक् , यदा रक्षति भूमिपः।।

— Shanti 67.35

16. त्रयी चान्वीक्षिकी चैव वार्ता च भरतर्षभ।

दण्डनीतिश्च विपुला विद्यास्तत्र निदर्शिताः।।

— Shanti 59.33

Compare—Arth-Shastra 1.2

— Manu 7.43

17. कृषिगोरक्षवाणिज्यंवैश्यकर्म स्वभावजम्।

— Geeta 18.44

18. पितृवत्पालयेद्वैश्यो युक्तः सर्वपशूनिह।
विकर्म तद्भवेदन्यत्कर्म यद्यत्समाचरेत्।
रक्षया हि तेषां वै महत्सुखमवाप्नुयात्।

— Shanti 60.22

19. Adiparvan 56.21

20. अभयं सत्त्वसंशुद्धिर्ज्ञानयोगव्यवस्थितिः।
दानं दमश्च यज्ञश्च स्वाध्यायस्तप आर्जवम्।।
अहिंसा सत्यमक्रोधस्त्यागः शान्तिरपैशुनम्।
दया भूतेष्वलोलुप्त्वं मार्दवं ह्रीरचापलम्।।
तेजः क्षमाः धृतिः शौचमद्रोहो नातिमानिता।
भवन्ति संपदं दैवीमभिजातस्य भारत।।

— Geeta XVI 1-3

21. दम्भो दर्पोऽभिमानश्च क्रोध पारुष्यमेव च।
अज्ञानं चाभिजातस्य पार्थ सम्पदासुरम्।।
प्रवृत्तिं च निवृत्तिं च जना न विदुरासुराः।
न शौचं नापि चाचारो न सत्यं तेषु विद्यते।।

— Geeta XVI. 4,6

22. काममाश्रित्य दुष्पूरं दम्भमानमदान्विताः।
मोहाद्गृहीत्वासद्ग्राहान्प्रवर्तन्तेऽशुचिव्रताः।।
चिन्तामपरिमेयां च प्रलयान्तामुपाश्रिताः।
कामोपभोगपरमा एतावदिति निश्चिताः।

— Geeta XVI. 10-11

6

Education for Values

In the Mahabharata period it was unimaginable that there could be any education without morals or virtues or values being part of it. "Dharma" was the centre for all the activities performed in the families as well as in the society. All individual, familial and societal activities were governed and justified within the broad parameters of Dharma. Moreover, God-devotion was the central thread of all virtues. The Acharyas were virtuous, religious and extremely devoted to their mission, might it be teaching, penancing, expiating or performing sacrifice for others. All the virtues used to be radiated to the disciples also. The teacher's every word and conduct had a direct and positive impact on the mind and the whole gamut of conduct, moral, social or academic, of the pupils. Simple living and high thinking was the order of the day.

New Concept

Value-education or Value-oriented Education is comparatively a modern term in the history of educational thought, which was popularly known earlier as Moral Education or Religious Education. It should be borne in mind that Value-oriented Education is a much broader and wider term than these two. Etymologically speaking the word "value" is derived from Greek word "valere", which literally means "good" and "beautiful". In the Mahabharata, the word "Dharma" is invariably used for any value or group of values or morals. In fact, the idea or belief, which will be good and beautiful, will be true also. Thus these three words-truth, beauty and good—are said to be the main components of any value or *sheel* or Dharma. In philosophic terms this trio is mentioned as Sachehidanand (Sat-Chit-Anand), a popular attributive used for God, Brahm, Atman, etc.

According to Annie Besant[1] there are four things which may be said to embody the main ideas of the life of a Brahamachari : service, study, simplicity and self-control. Self-control is said to be the vital centre of all the virtues or values. It means mastery of the body, guidance, training and management of the body, so that it may evolve into a useful and capable instrument, a good servant for life's work.

Some Aims for Religious Education

The pupils should :

1. have the opportunity to explore and understand the conceptual framework, rationality and structure of religion;
2. be shown how the religious dimension has influenced human experience both for good and bad;
3. recognise the significance of life with commitment to a religious faith has in the establishment of life-perspectives.
4. be offered the opportunity to explore the quality, values and dynamics of religious thought as manifested in the world's religious heritage—even if it is unlikely that pupils will appreciate the wealth, beauty and creative power within the faiths;
5. relearn their culture, bearing in mind that pupils may come from any group of society;
6. be educated for mutual respect and awareness, bearing in mind that rationality is relative to the parent culture and is largely socially determined;
7. be helped in their moral education, although one must remember that morality is only one constituent, part of religion and not its sum total;
8. develop such religious skills as :
   (a) the ability to interpret technical jargon;
   (b) the ability to interpret religious symbolism;
   (c) understanding the religious interpretation of an issue;
   (d) an awareness of religious phenomena and their significance;
   (e) enough knowledge to be able to give a "religious" answer to a problem.

Two Sets of Principles

With the advance of knowledge and socio-cultural phenomena, changes in Dharma had also been there. The followers of truth must have felt such changes necessary. In every Manvantara such changes had become necessary. Various Puranas declare that the Vedas themselves change from age to age. In this connection the verses[2] from the Matsya Puran are noteworthy.

It means that the Rishis with great concentration of mind study the Vedas. The Vedas formerly pronounced by Swayambhu have no beginning or end; and are divine. They change from age to age as the Dharma changes being compelled by their inner property of changing and the Dharma also changes from age to age as stated by the Vedas themselves. In fact there are two types of values-traditional or functional and eternal. Some of the traditional values, which might have been very significant in the past, may not be useful and relevant to the present time because some morals are subject to change from time to time and place to place. These values, which are subject to change, are called "Yuga Dharma" in our scriptures. The second type of values is known as "Sanatan Dharma" which consist of eternal and fundamental principles, which do not change in any time or place. Shruti is supposed to be of eternal nature while the Smriti is subject to change caused by various socio-cultural factors. Thus we come across two sets of principles :

1. A set of universal, eternal and fundamental principles.
2. A group of values derived from the first and finding expression in the individual and collective attitudes and behaviour.

The Mahabharata holds that the injunctions of the Vedas decline in the ages subsequent to those in which they are made, *i.e.* those injunctions are useless and not binding in the subsequent ages. For the Dharmas in the Krita, Treta, Dwapar, and Kali yugas are different, as they are dependent upon the strength of man. All this reveals that Manu and Saptarshis changed the Dharma wherever they found it necessary. Trayee, *i.e.* Shruti, remains unchanged. It is only Smriti which goes on changing.[3]

In the Manusmriti also the very distinction between the two sets of values has rightly been pointed out. It mentions that "there is one set of Dharmas for man in the Krita yuga, and a different set for each of Treta, Dwapar and Kali yugas. The Dharmas change according to the change of yugas". Dr. S. Radhakrishnan[4] has also rightly endorsed this very view. According to him, "The Hindu view makes room for essential changes. There must be no violent break with social heredity, and yet the new stresses, conflicts and confusions will have to be faced and overcome. While the truths of spirit are permanent, the rules change from age to age."

Hinduism

"Hinduism" is not a religion in terms of the popular sense of the word. Jawaharlal Nehru has very rightly observed that "Hinduism" as a faith is vague, amorphous, many-sided, all things to all men. It is hardly possible to define it, or needed to say definitely whether it is a religion or not, in the usual sense of the word. According to Dr. S. Radhakrishnan, Hindu religion can be described first in three words—"do the right". If it is taken to be true, it is applicable to all the faiths and religions. But the concept of right and wrong may differ from place to place, age to age and tradition to tradition.

Religion Defined

It is said that religion is a line of demarcation, which differentiates between the man-beast and the beast :

For if there be no mind
Debating good and evil,
And if religion send
No challenge to the will,
If only greed be there
For some material feast
How draw a line between
The man-beast and the beast?

—*Panchtantra*

Biologically speaking, man or woman has two inheritances—the first inheritance is physical while the second is cultural. According to Swami Ranganathanand, "It is this second inheritance that makes for the uniqueness of man; through it, man becomes capable of rising above his physical limitations and achieving unlimited personality expansion through the expansion of his awareness and sympathy. This highlights the importance of this second inheritance for education, ethics and religion." Thus the vertical growth in human personality has been the landmark in the history of mankind and has contributed greatly to the advancement of civilization and culture. Due to this change, a man has caused wonders in the areas of art, literature, knowledge, etc. In this context, *Julian Huxley's* following observation is noteworthy :

"*Man's evolution is not biological but psycho-social, it operates by the mechanism of cultural tradition, which involves the cumulative self-*

reproduction and self-variation of mental activities and their products. Accordingly, major steps in the human phase of evolution are achieved by break-through to new dominant patterns of mental organisation, of knowledge, ideas, and beliefs ideological instead of physiological or biological organization."

Really speaking values in isolation are meaningless, may they be ethical, social or spiritual. Ethics is inseparable from social context and social behaviour cannot be entirely devoid of ethics. Our ethical and moral values are vital integrating forces uniting man with man in society. Therefore, the real synonym of "Dharma" is "Integration" which has obviously two aspects — *abhyudaya* (social welfare) and *nishreyasa* (spiritual liberation). In the Mahabharata, therefore, "Dharma" is described it its aspect as "abhyudaya" as that which holds together, that which sustains all human beings :

"धारणात् धर्म इत्याहुः, धर्मो धारयति प्रजाः ।"

(Dharma holds and sustains; therefore, it is called Dharma. It holds the people together).

It is also said that wherefrom a man derives social welfare and spiritual liberation as well, that is to be called "Dharma"—

यतो वाऽभ्युदयनिश्रेयः सिद्धिः स धर्मः ।

(That which brings both earthly good and the supreme good in the form of salvation (Moksha) is Dharma.)

Essence of Dharma

The essence of Dharma lies in the right conduct which includes love, truth, non-violence, concern for others, equanimity of mind, etc. Out of a moral impulse and love for mankind, Jesus said, "Love thy neighbour as thyself" and Lord Krishna said, "You should help the poor".

Mohammad Paighamber asked his followers to ensure that no one is hungary to the right and left of their houses before they had their routine meals.

The Upnishads teach us about the futility of Karma (Karma kand=rituals) and advocate the importance of ethical qualities. But the Bhagavadgita[5] is emphatic in denouncing mere ritual. It strongly advocates the supreme necessity for developing Atma Gyan. Shankaracharya has been more particular in exposing the hollowness of rituals. He has emphatically proclaimed the significance of ethical qualities as the fundamental basis of spiritual life. The Mahabharata firmly holds that Dharma is the main shield of man. On being pleased with Yudhishthira, Yaksha wanted to revive the four Pandava princes. Overlooking his brothers like Bhima and Arjuna, Yudhishthir asked for the revival of Nakula so that Madri's one son may also survive. Yaksha asked, "Tell me as to why you choose Nakula rather than either of these two?" Yudhishthir replied, O yaksha, Dharma is the only shield of man and not Bhima or Arjuna. If Dharma is set at naught man will be ruined."

In the Mahabharata like other scriptures, good moral conduct has been described as the crux of Dharma. To one of the twentythree questions Yaksha (Yama, the God of death in disguise) asked Yudhishthir, "What makes one a real Brahmin? It is birth, good conduct or learning?" and told him to answer decisively. Yudhishthira's answer was crystal clear. He said emphatically, "Birth and learning do not make one a Brahmin. Good conduct alone does. However learned a person may be, he will not be a Brahmin if he is slave to bad habits. Even though he may be learned in the four Vedas, a man of bad conduct falls to a lower class."

While describing the path of righteousness (Dharma) it is said that one who works in the path of righteousness his very intention lends him virtue's greatness.[6] Lord Krishna has described himself as an everlasting source of righteousness.[7] In the Bhagavadgita, he tells Arjuna "Whenever there is a decline of righteousness and rise of unrighteousness, O Bharata, (Arjuna) then I send forth (create, incarnate) Myself. For the protection of the good, for the destruction of the wicked, for the establishment of righteousness, and I come into being from age to age."[8]

Divine and Devilish Traits

While describing the divine and demonial qualities of a person the Geeta[9] says that hypocrisy, pride's vain display, arrogance, anger, harsh and evil speech and ignorance are the attributes of a cursed one whereas, while describing the divine qualities, various moral and socio-cultural values have been enumerated as below :

Without fear and with life mind pure,
With self-control and in yogic wisdom sure,
With sacrifice and uprightness and with pious charity,
With love for the lore of scriptures and stern austerity.
With truth and non-violence and free from passion's fire,
With peace and renunciation and free from jealous desire,

Counting no one's faults and with compassion for all,
With fickle mind subdued, and gentle and modest withal.
Ever radiant and forgiving, with fortitude and purity of mind,
Without pride's vain excess and free from malice of any kind,
These, O Arjuna, are the attributes of the blessed one,
Born with divine nature. Indeed a heaven's son.[10]

From the Akhyan of Paravasu and Arvasu (sons of a great scholar Raibhya) and other episodes interwoven in the epic the conclusion is aptly derived that mere learning is not enough. Learning sans good conduct is just like a body without soul. Learning is one thing and virtue is quite another. One should know the difference between good and evil, if one is to seek good and shun evil, but this knowledge should soak into every thought and influence every act in one's life. Then indeed knowledge becomes virtue. The knowledge, that is merely so much undigested information crammed into the mind, cannot instill virtue.

Moral Values

The discussion of moral virtues is spread over various chapters of the Bhagavadgeeta. We might particularly mention four. In Ch. XII, we have a series of verses,[11] wherein God-devotion is regarded as the supreme virtue. In Ch. XIII we have five verses wherein the virtues are regarded as constituting knowledge.[12] In Ch. XVI we have got a full moral account of the divine heritage.

अभयं सत्त्वसंशुद्धिर्ज्ञानयोगव्यवस्थितिः ।
दानं दमश्च यज्ञश्च स्वाध्यायस्तप आर्जवम् । ।[13]

And finally, in Ch. XVIII, we have :

शमो दमस्तप शौचं क्षान्तिरार्जवमेव च ।
ज्ञानं विज्ञानमास्तिक्यं ब्रह्मकर्म स्वभावजम् । ।[14]

Further, we have an array of the most important moral virtues characterising the different social orders. **These are the** four main places **where the Bhagavadgita makes an analytical study of virtues.**

From the four loci-classici of the Bhagavadgeeta enumerated above, we find that an attempt has been particularly made in Ch. XII and XIII to centralise these virtues either in Devotion or in Knowledge-Bhakti or Jnana. If we read verses[15] from Ch. XII (16-19), we will see that all the moral virtues have been regarded there as exemplifications or specifications or exfoliations of the one central virtue of God-devotion. So Bhakti or God-devotion is the central virtue according to Ch. XII of the Bhagavadgita. In CH. XIII[16] it says almost in the spirit of Socrates that virtue alone constitutes knowledge. So this Socratic doctrine of virtue being knowledge and the other doctrine, namely, that all virtues are specifications of devotion, may be regarded as illustrations of the attempt of the Bhagavadgita to centralise all these virtues in a single principle.

Values or Virtues in Mahabharata (Geeta)

Ch. VI	1.	fearlessness
	2.	Control of Sense
	3.	Truthfulness
	4.	Absence of Anger
	5.	Kindness
	6.	Peace
	7.	Sacrifice
	8.	Valour
	9.	Absence of Malice
Ch.VII	1.	Control of Mind
	2.	Dutifulness
	3.	Lordliness
	4.	Service
	5.	Contentment
Ch. XII	1.	Compassion
	2.	Equanimity
	3.	Purity
	4.	Self-Control
	5.	Devotion
Ch. XIII	1.	Non-Violence
	2.	Free from Hypocrisy
	3.	Forgiveness
	4.	Straightforwardness
	5.	Non-Attachment

According to Aurobindo, "India's central conception is that of the Eternal, the spirit here incased in matter, involved and immanent in it an evolving on the material plane by rebirth of the individual up to the scale of being till in mental man it enters the world of ideas and realm of conscious morality, dharma. This achievement, this victory over unconscious matter develops its lines, enlarges its scope, elevates its level until the increasing manifestation of the sattvic or spiritual portion of the vehicle of mind enables the individual mental being in man to identify himself with the pure spiritual consciousness beyond Mind."

It is needless to say that India's social system and educational system, the latter a part (sub-system) of the former, are built upon this conception. Her philosophy formulates it, here religion is an aspiration to the spiritual consciousness and its fruits. Her art and literature have the same upward look. Her whole Dharma or law of being is founded upon it. **"यतो धर्मस्ततो जय:"** (where there is righteousness, victory is certain) It is the pet maxim of the great epic. R.C. Dutt, a noted translator of the epic, has rightly observed: "The real facts of the war had been obliterated by age. Legendary heroes had become the principal actors, and as is invariably the case in India, the thread of a high moral purpose, of the triumph of virtue and the subjugation of vice, was woven into the fabric of the great epic."[17] In this great epic religion is, very aptly, compared with a deep (lamp) wherein truth is the base, penance is like oil in it, and compassion and forgiveness are like its oil-stick and flame respectively. One must keep such a Lamp burning with great care.[18]

Development of Personality

For an all-round development of the personality, spiritual strength was considered of paramount significance. Physical and mental strength were definitely secondary. "Being" and "becoming" were considered to be involved in one and the same process but "to be" was considered nobler than "to do". For the upliftment of the self constant endeavour was considered essential so that non-self may be resisted and the self is upgraded. The Geeta says :

"Let self in him
Be raised by Self alone,
Let him not sink the self,
For, Self alone is self's true friend,
And Self alone is the foe of Self."[19]

Again

"The Self which has conquered self,
That alone is the friend of self,
But for him who cherishes non-Self,
The self itself becomes the foe."[20]

Exclusive devotion to the outward in one shape or the other endangers the inner Self of man, which alone gives him strength, beauty and distinction. "What does it profit a man, if he gains the whole world and loses his own soul?" asked the Prophet of Nazareth.

Many gain the world they seek. They then find to their cost that they have no power to make it their own.

The greatness of a man is not in what he does, but in what he was and what he "is" now. To be true to "one-self" is a higher service than serving others. The consecration of the Self to the task of attaining higher Self-hood is far, far nobler that acts which do not spring from this process. That is why Sri Krishna says :

"The Yogi is higher than the Ascetic,
He soars above the seers who know,
Higher than those who work too, is he,
Therefore, Arjuna, be thou a Yogi."[21]

Rules of Conduct

Hermitage or Ashram was an institution in ancient India in which moral and spiritual discipline was learnt and practised. It is true that rigid rules were laid down for the conduct of pupils. In addition to making good manners obligatory, these rules had a hygienic, moral and religious background and significance.

The student was required to bathe daily, to avoid honey, meat and all pungent foods, perfumes, garlands, ointments and such other luxuries were also denied to him. Even if he was very rich and his father could afford to keep a carriage, as long as he was a student, he was not supposed to use it. Other amenities such a shoes, umbrellas, etc., were also prohibited. "Tongue, arms and stomach" were to be kept under control. All evil habits such as spitting, yawning, breaking into peals of laughter, cracking the joints of the fingers were strictly forbidden. Those who gambled, those who treated animals cruelly and those who used spirituous liquors were severely dealt with. While performing his devotions, the student was enjoined to stand silently in the morning and "sit during the evening from the time when one light was visible until the other light disappeared".

These rules of conduct are indicative of the fact that during the epic period great strees was laid on etiquette and good manners. It was firmly believed that manners take the shape of habits, second nature of an individual. The habits, good or bad, go a long way in shaping one's character.

The Mahabharata is replete with such noble illustrations (like Nala, Savitri, etc.) which inspire India's sons and daughters today as they did in generations past. Its moral standards are unparalleled elsewhere, and its message deserves to be imbibed, particularly by a war-dominated world like ours. The cause of conflict appears everywhere as a claim for something higher than a mere clod of earth; yet more often than not, such pretensions are only a cloak to cover the covetousness of land and power-hungry casuists who dare not admit the truth even to themselves. Nevertheless, "there is a divinity that shapes our ends", and Vyasa conveys to us the encouraging assurance that Truth and Righteousness ultimately prevail over all the pretensions of power and deceit. At the end of the epic he conveys the gist of his message as under :

"O, my son listen to the essence of Dharma and having heard it you should inculcate it in your own practical life. Never do unto others which you may not like for yourself.[22]

Compare,

> "This above all-to thine ownself be true,
> And it must follow, as the night the day,
> That thou not then be false to any man."
>
> —Shakespeare (*Hamlet*).

Footnotes

1. Hindu Ideals, Adyar, p. 28
2. ऋषयस्तपसा वेदानहोरात्रमधीयते।
   अनादिनिधना दिव्याः पूर्वप्रोक्ता स्वयंभुवा।।
   स्वधर्मसंवृताः सांगा यथाधर्म युगे युगे।
   विक्रियन्ते स्वधर्म तु वेदवेदाद्यथायुगम्।।

   —Matsya Puran 142.48-49
3. वेदवादाश्चानुयुगं ह्रसन्तीति नः श्रुतम्।।
   अन्ये कृतयुगे धर्माः त्रेतायां द्वापरे परे।
   अन्ये कलियुगे चैव यथाशक्तिकृता इव ।।

   —Shanti 260.7-8

   Compare
   अन्ये कृतयुगे धर्माः त्रेतायां द्वापरे अपरे।
   अन्ये कलियुगे नृणां युगह्रासानुरुपतः।।

   —Manu 1.85

4. *Religion and Soceity,* p.113
5. The Bhaghavadgita II 42—46, IX 20-21
6. *Ibid.* VI.40
7. *Ibid.* XIV. 27
8. *Ibid.* IV. 7-8
9. *Ibid.* XVI. 4
10. *Ibid.* XVI 1—3
11. The verses begin with

    अद्वेष्टा सर्वभूतानां मैत्र करुण एव च।
    निर्ममो निरहंकारः समदुःखसुखः क्षमी।।

    Ibid. XII. 13
12. अमानित्वमदम्भित्वमहिंसा क्षान्तिरार्जवम्।
    आचार्योपासनं शौचं स्थैर्यमात्मविनिग्रहः।।

    Ibid. XIII.7

    (Absence of pride, freedom from hypocrisy, non-violence, forgiveness, straightforwardness, service of the preceptor, purity of mind and body, steadfastness, self-control)
13. *Ibid.* XVI. 1
14. *Ibid.* XVIII. 42
15. अनपेक्षः शुचिर्दक्षः उदासीनो गतव्यथः।
    सर्वारम्भपरित्यागी योमद्भक्तः स मे प्रियः।।
    यो न हृष्यति न द्वेष्टि न शोचति न काङ्क्षति।
    शुभाशुभपरित्यागी भक्तिमान्यः स मे प्रियः।।
    समः शत्रौ च मित्रे च तथा मानापमानयोः।
    शीतोष्णसुखदुःखेषु समः संगविवर्जितः।।
    तुल्यनिन्दास्तुतिर्मौनी संतुष्टो येन केनचित्।
    अनिकेतः स्थिरमतिभक्तिमान्मे प्रियो नरः।।

    Ibid. XII. 16—19
16. अध्यात्मज्ञाननित्यत्वं तत्त्वज्ञानार्थदर्शनम्।
    एतज्ज्ञानमिति प्रोक्तमज्ञानं यदतोऽन्यथा।।

    XIII. 11

    [Fixity in self-knowledge, observing everywhere the object of true knowledge (God); all this is declared to be knowledge (wisdom); which contrary to this is called ignorance.]
17. *The Mahabharata* (condensed into English verse), Translator's Epilogue, p.177 (Jaico)
18. सत्याधारस्तपस्तैलं दया वर्ति क्षमा शिखा।
    अन्धकारे प्रवेष्टव्ये दीपो यत्नेन वार्यताम्।।
19. उध्दरेदात्मनाऽऽत्मानं नात्मानमवसादयेत्।
    आत्मैव ह्यात्मनो बन्धुरात्मैव रिपुरात्मनः।।

    —Geeta VI.6

20. बन्धुरात्मानस्तस्य येनात्मैवात्मना जितः।
अनात्मनस्तु शत्रुत्वे वर्तेतात्मैव शत्रुवत्।।

—Geeta, VI. 5

21. तपस्विभ्यऽधिको योगी ज्ञानिभ्योऽपि मतोऽधिकः।
कर्मिभ्यश्चाधिको योगी तस्माद्योगी भवार्जुन।।

—Geeta, VI. 46

7

Righteousness : A Code of Conduct

Victory is certain, O mind!
Away with false fear,
Devotion bears its fruits,
Shoulders we have,
Broad and strong,
And intelligence
We can gather what we work for
Unalterable law protects
Our efforts unfagging
Away then with fear and despondency!

—*Mahabharata*

Law of Karma

The great epic Mahabharata has clearly proclaimed, "Yato Dharmastato Jayah" (Victory lies there, where righteousness dwells). The epic has expressly indicated that the safest and the surest path leading to success in life is righteousness and performance of one's duty. It is true that a righteous person has to suffer sometimes, and the unrighteous enjoy. But it is not a permanent feature. It is only a question of time. "As you sow, so you shall you reap", is a saying based on the age-old experiences of mankind which formulate the law of Karma. One is bound to reap the consequences of one's good or bad deeds and words. At many places doubts have been raised on this count. But ultimately we find that such doubts are reconciled by the virtue of various episodes and side stories interwoven in the epics. Therefore, under no circumstances should one deviate from the path of righteousness; but perform duties to the best of one's ability.

Cause-and-Effect Relationship

In fact everyone knows from experience and without the help of any doctrine that every thought or act, good or bad, has at once its effect on oneself, apart from its effect on others or on the outside world. Every motion of the mind deals a stroke, as with a hammer, on character and whether one wants it or not, alters its shape for better or worse. Thus man is continuously shaping his own self by the virtue of his good or bad Karmas. However, the Law of Karma does not support the doctrine of predestination. According to Dr. Radhakrishnan, "In our relations with human failures, belief in Karma inclines us to take a sympathetic attitude and develop reverence before the mystery of misfortune. The more understanding we are, the less do we pride ourselves on our superiority. Faith in Karma induces in us the mood of true justice or charity which is the essence of spirituality. We realize how infinitely helpless and frail human beings are. When we look at the warped lives of the poor, we see how much the Law of Karma is true. If they are lazy and criminal, let us ask what chance they had of choosing to be different. They are more unfortunate than wicked. Again, failures are due not so much to "sin" as to errors which lead us to our doom. In Greek tragedy man is held individually less responsible and circumstances or the decisions of Moira more so. The tale of Oedipus Rex tells us how he could not avoid his fate to kill his father and marry his mother, in spite of his best efforts. The parting of Hector and Andromancy in Homer is another illustration. In Shakespeare again, we see the artist leading on his characters to their destined ends by what seems a very natural development of their foibles, criminal folly in Lear or personal ambition in Macbeth."[1]

It is said that "exertion is a powerful weapon". From the illustrations of sufferings and trials of the Pandavas, and Draupadi, Rama, Lakshmana and Sita, during their exile, the above saying stands well-testified. We should accept the challenges of life and perform our duties expected of us. Here lies the path towards peace of mind. It has been well said by Lakshmana, "Have faith and trust in God, pursue virtue and engage in action."

Opposites of Life

The Ramayana and Mahabharata are superb in the delineation of day-to-day life, its pleasures and pains, joys and sorrows and the complexity of functioning of human mind and heart. Devotion and submission of the self to the cosmic self are the central values of the epics. The devotion and

1. An Idealist View of Life, p.222

obedience of a son, suffering and sacrifice of a mother, trials and endurance of various heroes and heroines, maintenance of chastity at the cost of one's life, jealousies of co-wives, intrigues of inner apartments, dedication and devotion of a servant, lamentation of a wife over the death of husband, valour and bravery of the soldiers—these all have been depicted with a great literary acumen.

Keeping in view the uniqueness of these two epics of ancient India, the Ramayana and Mahabharata, late Jawaharlal Nehru has rightly remarked in his "Discovery of India", I do not know any book anywhere which has exercised such a continuous and pervasive influence on the mass mind as these two. Dating back to a remote antiquity, they are still a living force in the life of the Indian people." In true sense they are national epics of India, because no work of this antiquity could influence various spheres of Indian life. Almost all spheres, *i.e.* art, architecture, literature, religion, life-style, socio-political thoughts, etc., all the areas stand deeply influenced by these epics. As far as literature is concerned these epics had left a deep impact on almost each and every form of literature in terms of style, contents, emotion, imagination, etc. The characters of these epics still inspire us to face various challenges of life with full confidence and patience.

Characters : Our Guiding Stars

Ramayana is the premier epic of India which is appropriately called "Adi Kavya". On the one hand, it holds very great literary merit and, on the other, it is a treatise of our moral, social and religious values having the capacity to guide a man for happy living as a member of the family and the society at large. It also provides very good tips on statecraft. Its various episodes and side stories serve a didactic purpose also. Study of the Ramayana and Mahabharata gives joy par excellence for the literary persons and synchronically conveys the message of righteous conduct. In the Ramayana, we observe various duties of rulers, ruled, parents, children, brothers, sisters, friends, servants, teachers and taughts, etc., in a most appealing manner. Desire, greed, lust, jealousy, anger and arrogance—these are called six enemies of man. People from all strata of society fall prey to these enemies. These are the root cause of the sufferings of man. Kaikeyi fell prey to greed and lost not only her reputation in the royal family and elsewhere but also her husband. Surpanakha and Ravana are the examples of the victims of lust.

At many places the Ramayana illustrates triumph of righteousness over the forces of evil. Rama is a symbol of righteousness whereas Ravana is a symbol of evil forces. The struggles of Rama during his exile and his overcoming of all the odds and obstacles inspire us to make sustained efforts against the evil forces even in the most adverse circumstances. The doctrine of Karma and other worldliness are apparently visualized in the epic. The purity and sanctity of the intention and purpose are bound to lead to good results—this is a simple philosophy reflected in all the characters of the Ramayana and Mahabharata.

The message of the Mahabharata is the message of truth and righteousness. Its characters have symbolic importance also—blind king Dhritrashtra represents ignorance, Yudhishthir represents righteousness, while Duryodhana represents unrighteousness like Ravana, Arjuna, the individual soul, and Lord Krishna, the supreme soul. Kurukshetra, where the mighty battle was fought, represents our mind. Such symbolism reflecting a variety of positive and negative human values has universal significance. Observe the natural prediction of Bhishma against Duryodhan,

Deaf to wisdom's voice, Duryodhan,
Deaf to parents and to kin,
Thou shall perish in thy folly
In the unrepented sin!

Lastly unrighteousness (Duryodhana) perishes and righteousness (Yudhishthir) comes out victor.

In the Ramayana, Ram has been depicted as an embodiment of various ethical values like generosity, compassion, forgiveness, absence of jealousy and anger, truthfulness, pleasant speaking, non-discrimination on the count of status or riches, honouring one's pledge at all costs, peace, humanity, etc. In the epic, there are various references to several postulates of our culture. Of these, one of the prominent one is the power of destiny which has been shown as all-pervading and influencing the lives of the people. The chain of events happened immediately before and after the announcement of anointment of Rama to throne clearly indicates the all-pervasive power of destiny. In the Mahabharata also there are a number of episodes revealing the power of destiny.

We find various portraits of superhumans in the Ramayana like Rama, Vishwamitra, Kaushalya, etc., who were human beings also, and being so, were not above human weaknesses. The epic illustrates that even superhuman beings like Rama, Vishwamitra, Parasuram, etc., were having various weaknesses. This reflects the realistic attitude of the epic. The principle of equanimity, as described in the Bhagavadgita, has been depicted in various characters of the Ramayana. The epic preaches that we should not exaggerate our difficulties or show our helplessness in adverse circumstances. But we should be even minded in joy and sorrow, victory and defeat, pleasure and pain, prosperity and poverty, etc. Then only we will be able to overcome the difficulties and achieve success in life. In all odds and obstacles, one should maintain self-control.

For the peaceful and harmonious life, the fulfilment of the four ends of life, *i.e.* Dharma (righteousness and duty), Artha (material prosperity), Kama (legitimate sex and other pleasures) and Moksha (liberation of soul), is essential. In both the epics, Ramayana and Mahabharata we find that a very high sense of righteousness and duty has been observed even during the war-time. The norms of warcraft were strictly observed even in very precarious moments.

The central theme of the Ramayana is the noble and sublime character of Rama. He was kind, generous, brave, considerate, pleasant, softspoken, brief-spoken but first to speak, unsuspecting, free from jealousy, forgiver of others' faults, full of gratitude and righteous. He always honoured his word. Deep respect for elders, especially parents, rigid adherence to monogamy and a stern sense of duty were his outstanding qualities.

Ritualism vs. Righteousness

Nothing is good or bad in itself. It is the inner spirit of any action or reaction which decides its merit of virtue or otherwise. The epics tell us at many places in many contexts that actions should not be evaluated or judged on the basis of their surface value. Similarly, to testify the merit of religious experience, it is essential that the evidence should come from the one who has had it himself. The evidence of one without such experiences is worthless. In fact the religious experience of only such an agent who has himself undergone the experience can justify whether the religious experience does what is claimed for it.

Of course, religious experience is not a knowledge which can be publicly verified and proved. "Seeing is believing" does not apply to the religious experience. It is the example par excellence of faith and faith cannot be identified with knowledge. It is rightly said that "faith asserts, science proves its assertion and one of the most important assertions of faith is that some assertions can be proved scientifically. But certain episodes given in the epics are just symbolic. The content and themes of these episodes cannot be proved scientifically. The story of the mongoose interwoven in the Mahabharata is one of this character which reveals the difference between the two types of charity—that of King Yudhishthir observed during his Ashwamedh Yajnya (horse sacrifice) and of a hungry Brahman of Kurukshetra who gave his bowl of flour to another hungry Brahman, who had come to him as a guest.

The charity and generosity of Yudhishthir had touched new heights during his Ashwamedha Yajnya. Food and clothes, gold and pearls were given away by Yudhishthir. It is said that no one had heard even in a story of such bounty given before, nor would future Kings easily achieve such generosity. Nevertheless when the mongoose entered into the magnificent pavilion of sacrifice and took a round, he was utterly disappointed. The mongoose, in disgust, laughed and told Yudhishthir plainly, "All your celebration is not equal to a bowl of flour once given away where I live in Kurukshetra."

When, in spite of the best treatment, the mongoose was not satisfied and went on passing derisory remarks, Yudhishthir asked him the cause of disappointment and also as to why half of his body was all golden and bright. On this the mongoose narrated the following story in the pavilion in the presence of a number of kings and assembled priests :

"Long before you waged your battle there, a Brahmana lived in Kurukshetra, who obtained his daily food by gleaning in the fields. He and his wife, son and daughter in-law, all four lived in this manner. Every day in the afternoon they would sit down and have their only meal for the day. On days when they failed to find enough grain, they would fast until the next afternoon. They would not keep over anything for the next day if they got more than they required for the day. This was the strict *unchhavritti* discipline they had pledged themselves to observe.

"They passed their days thus for many years, when a great drought came and there was famine all over the land. All cultivation ceased and there was neither sowing nor harvesting nor any grain scattered in the fields to be gleaned. For many days the Brahmana and his family starved. One day, after wandering in hunger and heat, with great difficulty they came home with a small quantity of maize which they had gathered. They ground it and after saying their prayers they divided the flour into four equal parts and, offering thanks to God, sat down eagerly to eat. Just then, a Brahmana entered and he was exceedingly hungry. Seeing an unexpected guest arrive, they got up and made due obeisance and asked him to join them. The pure-souled Brahmana and his wife and son and daughter-in-law were exceedingly delighted to have the good fortune of receiving a guest at that juncture. 'O best of Brahmanas, I am a poor man. This flour of maize was obtained in accordance with Dharma. Pray accept this. May blessings attend to you', said the Brahmana of Kurukshetra and gave his share of the flour to the guest. The guest ate it with avidity but he was still hungry when he had finished.

"Seeing his hungry and unsatisfied look, the Brahmana was grieved and did not know what to do, when his wife said : 'Lord, give my share also to him. I shall be glad if the guest's hunger be satisfied.' Saying this, she handed her share of the flour to her husband to be given to the guest.

"Faithful one, said the Brahmana, 'the beasts and the birds and all the animals tend the females of their species with care. May man do worse? I cannot accept your suggestion. What shall I gain this or in the other world if I leave you to starve and suffer hunger, you who help me and serve me to do the sacred duties of a householder's life? Beloved one, you are now skin and bone and famished and exceedingly hungry. How can I leave you to suffer in that condition and hope to attain any good by feeding the guest? No, I cannot accept your offer.'

"You are versed in the shastras, best of Brahmanas', replied the wife. 'Is it not true that Dharma, Artha and all the objects of human activity are to the common and equal benefit of both of us who have been joined together? Do look on me with compassion and take my share of the flour and satisfy the requirements of this our guest. You are hungry as I am and you should not make any distinction between us. I entreat you not to deny my request.'

"The Brahmana yielded and took the wife's share and gave it to the guest who took it greedily and ate it. But he was still hungry! Great was the distress of the poor Brahmana of Kurukshetra. His son, who saw this, came forward. 'Father, here is my share,' said he. 'Give it to this guest who seems to be still hungry. I shall be indeed happy if we shall thus be able to fulfil our duty.'

"The father's distress increased. 'Child!' he exclaimed, 'old men can stand starvation. Youth's hunger is severe. I am not able to find it in my heart to accept what you say.'

"The son insisted : 'It is the duty of the son to look after his father in his declining years. The son is not different from the father. Is it not said that the father is born afresh in his son? My share of the flour is yours in truth. I beg of you to accept what I give and feed this hungry guest.'

"Dear boy, your nobility and your mastery over the senses fill me with pride. Blessing on you; I shall accept your share!' said the father, and he took the son's flour and gave it to the guest to eat. The guest ate the third part of the flour also but he was still hungry! The Brahmana, who lived on scattered grain, was confused.

"While he was in distress, not knowing what to do, his daughter-in-law addressed him thus :

'Lord, I shall give my share too and gladly complete our efforts to feed this guest. I beg of you to accept it and bless me, your child, for, by that, I shall have eternal good as my reward.'

"The father-in-law was sad beyond measure. 'O girl of spotless character, pale and emaciated as you are from starvation, you propose to give your part of the food also to me, so that I may earn merit by giving it to this guest. If I accept your offer, I shall indeed be guilty of cruelty. How could I possibly look on when you wither in hunger?'

"The girl would not listen. 'Father, you are lord of my lord and master, preceptor of my preceptor, god of my god. I implore you to accept my flour. Is not this body of mine dedicated wholly to serve my lord? You should help me to attain the good. Do take this flour, I entreat you.'

"Thus implored by his daughter-in-law, the Brahmana accepted her share of the flour and blessed her saying, 'Loyal girl, may every good be yours!'

"The guest received this last portion avidly and ate it and was satisfied.

"Blessed is your hospitality, given with the purest intention and to the uttermost of your capacity. Your gift has pleased me. Lo there! the gods are showering flowers in admiration of your extraordinary sacrifice. See! the gods and the gandharvas have come down in their bright chariots with their attendants to take you with your family to the happy regions above. Your gift has achieved swarga for you, as well as for your ancestors. Hunger destroys the understanding of men. It makes them go aside from the path of rectitude. It leads them to evil thoughts. The pious, when suffering the pangs of hunger, lose their steadfastness. But you have, even when hungry, bravely set aside your attachment to wife and son and placed Dharma above all else. Rajasuya sacrifices and horse sacrifices completed in splendor would pale into insignificance before the great sacrifice you have done through this single act of hospitality. The chariot is waiting for you. Enter and go to swarga, you and your family'. Saying this the mysterious guest disappeared."

Having related this story of the Kurukshetra Brahmana who lived by gleaning scattered ears of corn in the field, the mongoose continued :

"I was nearby and caught the fragrance wafted from that flour of the Brahmana. It made my head all gold. I then went and rolled in joy on the ground where some of the flour had been scattered. It made one side of me into bright gold. I turned on the other side but there was no more flour left and that part of me is still as it was. Desirous of getting my body made all gold, I have been trying every place where men perform great yajnas and penances. I heard that Yudhishthir of world fame was performing a yajna and came here, believing that this sacrifice might come up to the standard. But I found it did not. So, I said that your great ashwamedha was not so great as the gift of flour which that Brahmana made to his guest." The mongoose then disappeared.

Charity Analyzed

In the above story we see that the charity of the King Yudhishthir and that of the Brahman of Kurukshetra are poles apart. There cannot be any comparison as far as material gifts are concerned. The Ashwamedha sacrifice was completed in accordance with the injunctions of shastras. Everyone who had come to that Yajnya was duly attended to and accorded suitable honours and gifts. Everyone was pleased with the gifts and returned happy and contended. But still the charity of the Brahman of Kurukshetra was more significant and pious than that of King Yudhishthira's bounteous gifts because they were less weighty in the following terms :

1. Purity and sanctity of intention;
2. Intensity of involvement of the self; and
3. Quantity of sacrifice involved in the charity.

Principle of Will

Amongst the above criteria the purity and sanctity of the intention or purpose of the doer is the most significant one, which merit the intensity of righteousness of any individual or social action. If we apply this criterion and compare the great deeds of Drona, Arjuna and Eklavya, in terms of archery, we can say that Eklavya was greater even than Drona and Arjuna. Drona was appointed by Bhishma to instruct the princes in the use of arms, so he gave training in arms to the princes to earn his livelihood and fame. Arjuna, a great exponent of archery and the most favourite disciple of Drona, learnt archery in order to be a great king by conquering other States and expand the empire whereas the purpose of Eklavya who modelled an idol of Drona and learnt archery at his feet taking him as real guru since he, being a tribal boy, was not accepted as disciple by Drona, was to protect the lives of the deers and other hermit-mates from the wild animals.

The difference of degree in the purity and sanctity of purpose or intention in all the three examples quoted is quite apparent. The intention or purpose of being a good archer in the case of Eklavya was far superior and the most pious and pure as compared to the purpose of Drona or Arjuna of being a good archer. Keeping in view this criterion, we can say that Eklavya was greater than Drona and Arjuna.

Similarly in the above-narrated story of the mongoose, we find that the purpose of performing Ashwamedha Yajnya (horse sacrifice) by Yudhishthir was to subdue the kings by establishing his supremacy and add further splendour and grandeur to his empire whereas the intention of the Brahman of Kurukshetra in giving a bowl of flour to a hungry Brahman was quite pious and his sacrifice in this very charity was very weighty as compared to the bounteous gifts of Yudhishthir; because the donor Brahman and other members of his family were themselves starving. They honoured the Brahman guest at the cost of their own hunger. Truly speaking no comparison is possible between the two sacrifices, *i.e.* one of the king Yudhishthir and the other of the hungry Brahman of Kurukshetra. That is why in the eyes of the mongoose the magnificent horse sacrifice of the king Yudhishthir was vain because it could not get half of his body converted into golden and shining one whereas half of his body had already become golden simply by rolling in the granules of flour which had fallen on the ground while a Brahman was giving flour in charity to a hungry Brahman.

Yudhishthir's action (charity) was with a specific purpose whereas the Brahman's action was without any specific purpose. In the words of Immanuel Kant, a noted idealist philosopher, we can call the act of the Brahman as "Principle of the will" without regard to the ends. Technically speaking the words, purpose and intention used above sound two different connotations. The "purpose" of an act comprises the expected result or results for the sake of which it is done. The word intention contrasts with "consequences", whereas "purpose" does not. The word "purpose" conveys a comparatively narrower sense than "intention". Otherwise these two words do not contrast with each other. While discussing the supreme principle of morality Kant's following observation is quite pertinent with the theme of the episode cited above, *i.e.* an action without regard to the ends :

> That an action done from duty derives its moral worth, not from the purpose which is to be attained by it, but from the maxim by which it is determined, and therefore does not depend on the realization of the object of the action, but merely on the principle

of volition by which the action has taken place, without regard to any object of desire. It is clear from what precedes that the purpose which we may have in view in our actions, or their effects regarded as ends and springs of the will, cannot give to actions any unconditional or moral worth. In what, then, can their worth lie if it is not to consist in the will and in reference to its expected effect? It cannot lie anywhere but in the principle of the will without regard to the ends which can be attained by the action.

Conclusion

As we have already observed, "Yato Dharmastato Jayah" is the pet maxim of the great epic. Therefore, to confirm and reconfirm the testimony of this maxim good many thematic episodes have been interwoven in the epic in one context or the other. In this regard the following episodes are noteworthy :

1. Episode of Astik (Adi.)
2. Meeting Chitrarath (Adi.)
3. Burning of Wax-house (Adi.)
4. Assassination of Jarasandh (Sabha)
5. Killing of Shishupal (Sabha)
6. Duet with Yaksha (Van.)
7. Killing of Kichak (Virat.)

Righteousness includes a variety of spiritual moral, ethical, social and cultural values. In every story/episode the message regarding one value or the other is communicated. In many episodes like "Yaksha-prishna" a number of values together have been highlighted. Presenting models through self-conduct is all the more important than teaching others. That is why, in "Yaksha Prishna", it has been clearly said, "The setting of religious standards for others is hypocrisy." Swami Dayanand has rightly said that "Fraud and hypocrisy mean having one thing in mind and quite the reverse outside, cheating others and serving one's selfish end without minding the injury done to others." This is just opposite to righteousness. The Mahabharata has a universal message on Dharma (righteousness) for all the people of the world. It loudly proclaims that not at the cost of fear, greed or even life should Dharma be surrendered. This is the ultimate teaching of the Mahabharata which declares, "One should never do that to another which one regards injurious to one's ownself." This is the true essence of Dharma observed in all the religions of the world. In Indian culture the height of righteousness was to such an extent that people used to sacrifice their own life for the weal of others. Philanthropy has been a distinguishing quality of great personalities. One such great king expresses his heart's desire as under :

न त्वहं कामये राज्यं न स्वर्गं नापुनर्भवम्।
कामये दुःखतप्तानां प्राणिनामार्तिनाशनम्।।

(I covet not temporal power,
Nay, nor heaven, nor even
Freedom from the cycle of life,
I pray only that those sunk in distress
From their agony be redeemed.)

8

Education for Women

Deteriorating Trend

Educational development of women as depicted in the Mahabharata reveals that women were not given adequate opportunities for the development of their personalties. While tracing the reasons of backwardness of women in education, we find that their overall social status was mainly responsible for this. Their field was mainly household. They were not supposed to earn the livelihood. In the prevailing social phenomena, they were not safe. There was every fear of atrocities by enemies or abduction by dacoits. Under such circumstances. It was not considered wise to send girls to the hermitages located in far-flung forest areas. Therefore, as far as possible, their education was arranged at home only.

According to Altekar[1] education of women prevailed in the Vedic society. But by the time of the Mahabharata the tradition of study of the Vedas by the women folk was almost extinct. This very phenomena is indicative of the degeneration of the then civilization. It was mostly confirmed opinion of the people that the knowledge of scriptures was not essential for women.

Safety Problem

Again security problem seems to be one of the reasons, as said above, for depriving women from the study of the Vedas and allied scriptures. However, inspite of certain restrictions and lack of safety, some women used to study the Vedas. In the Mahabharata many women are said to have learnt by heart many hymns and prayers from the Vedas. Vinata blessed Garuda by reciting Vedic verses. While deserting "Karna" Kunti prayed[2] for his welfare and recited Vedic mantras.

Socio-Religious Status

In the Rigved[3] it is mentioned that couple, who perform sacrifices and offer prayers with harmonious minds, always become happy. It was a common belief that the mental make-up and conduct of a child is influenced by his parentage. Therefore, the right of learning the Vedas and performing Agnihotra was given to women. They deserve initiation (Maunji-bandhan) also, as Nirnaya-Sindhu puts it.[4]

Theoretically the Mahabharata holds that women have the right not only for learning but teaching also. There is good evidence to testify to this notion. There is a reference of Brahmni (female Brahmin) named "Shiva",[5] who studied all the Vedas and having practised penances attained salvation.

Similarly there was a Brahmini Siddha[6] who attained the heavenly abode by the virtue of her celebacy and yogic practices. In Shanti Parvan there is a famous episode of Sulbha, who debates with Janaka on various subtle issues of spirituality and introduces herself to Janak in the following manner.

प्रधानो नाम राजर्षिव्यक्त ते श्रोत्रमागतः।
कुले तस्य समुत्पन्नां सुलभां नाम विद्धि माम्।।
साहं तस्य कुले जाता भर्तर्यसति मद्विधे।
विनीता मोक्षधर्मेषु चराम्येका मुनिव्रतम्।।

("I am Sulbha, born in the noble family of the king named Pradhan. Since I could not get a suitable match, I learnt the Vedas and other sacred scriptures from learned scholars and now I follow Moksha and other sacred vows."[7])

Formal vs. Non-Formal Education

In general, girls used to have non-formal education from elder brothers, parents, learned guests, etc. King Drupad had appointed a learned Brahmin to teach statecraft to his son. His daughter (Draupadi) also learnt Brihaspathi-Artha-shastra from a learned Brahman at home.[8] Shakuni, the Prince of Gandhar and Gandhari (sister of Shakuni) were both well-versed in the Arthshastra.[9] Though the girls were not sent to hermitages, they were sent to stay with some female members used to live which included the Guru's wife, daughters, etc.[10]

Muni Durwasa, being pleased with the hospitability of Kunti, at her father's (Kuntibhoj) house, trained her in the effective use of the "Atharva-shiras" mantra.[11] By the virtue of this very mantra, it is said, Kunti pleased various gods and got three sons—Yudhishthir, Bhima and Arjuna. Madri followed in the footsteps of Kunti and pleased the twin-gods (Ashwini) and got twin sons—Nakula and Sahdev.

From the above description, it is clear that though the girls were not sent to the hermitages, for princesses and women-folk of hermitages such occasions were not rare when they received knowledge of the Vedas and other scriptures through learned fathers, brothers or other scholarly guests. They also used to develop their knowledge and understanding by listening to the discourses of sages and other scholars from time to time particularly on occasions of certain ceremonies including various sacrifices, etc. In ordinary families also traveller guests used to tell various interesting stories pertaining to the various places they had travelled through. In village "Ekchakra" where the Pandavas lived in disguise with their mother (Kunti), a Brahmin had narrated various interesting stories to Kunti.[12] Shakuntala living in the hermitage of Kanva came to know about her parentage by hearing a conversation between the sage Kanva and a traveller guest.

Women used to take keen interest in narrating and listening to stories. This was not only a source of entertainment for them but also a book of knowledge. Brihannala (name adopted by Arjuna in disguise in the kingdom of Virata) used to narrate various interesting stories and amuse the ladies in the inner apartment of King Virata.

Special Tutors

In affluent families or royal families special tutors were appointed to teach the girls. In the palace of Virata Brihannala was entrusted with the duties of training the females in the fine arts like dance, singing, music, etc.[13]

From this singular evidence available in the Mahabharata it appears that the appointment of male teachers for girls was not appreciated. This is why King Virata got the impotency of Brihannala ensured before assigning him the job. In the joint families the girls used to get practical lessons in various useful matters before their marriage from their father, mother and other elderly women available in the family. Kunti[14] and Gandhari[15] had educated their daughters and also daughters-in-law in the religious conduct, household management, their respective duties towards other members of the family, etc.

Arts and Crafts

The data available in the Mahabharata reveals that women's education was almost informal. There were no formal agencies of education for them. The attributive "चतुष्षष्ठिविशारदाः" used for maid-servants of Yudhishthir indicates that they were well-versed in all the 64 arts mentioned in "Kamasutra" and other treatises. They must have learnt these arts informally only. In such informal education, women used to learn all that was required for leading a happy married life, but at times, because of emotionality, they ignored their duties. Because of such non-informal education, they were generally found to be good at heart but they lacked rational temper at times. Being invoked with 'Pativrit Dharma' Gandhari used to have her eyes entied with a piece of cloth (because her husband was blind). By doing so she neglected her duties as a mother. Had she not done so she could have reared her children in a proper manner and cultivated in them the desired social and spiritual values.

In his famous treatise, "Education in Ancient India" Dr. A. S. Altekar rightly observed:—"In the heyday of her glory education in India was broad-based." Women and ordinary people were allowed to derive the maximum benefits from it. Although it would not be fair to compare "the scanty remains of a bygone system" with the tremendous advance that the West has made in our times, it can be said that the education during the epic period "developed character and personality. It included civic virtues, introduced a high standard of culture and emphasised the necessity of self-imposed discipline and stern regard for duty".

Footnotes

1. Dr. A.S. Altekar, *Position of women in Ancient India* p.10
2. स्वस्ति तेऽस्त्यन्तरिक्षेभ्यश्च पार्थिवेभ्यश्च पुत्रक।
   दिवेभ्यश्चैव भूतेभ्यस्तथा तोयचराश्च ये।।
   —Aranyak 292.10-14
3. या दम्पती सुमनसा सुनुत आ च धावतः।
   देवासो नित्ययाऽशिरा।
   —ऋक् 8.31.51
4. पुराकल्पे तु नारीणां मौञ्जीबन्धनमिष्यते।
   अध्यापनं च वेदानां सावित्रीवाचनं तथा।।
   —Nirnay Sindhu

5. अत्र सिध्दा शिवा नाम ब्राह्मणी वेदपारगा।
अधीत्य सकलान् वेदान् लेभेऽसन्देहमक्षयम्।।
—Udyog 190.18
6. Shalya Parvan 54.6
7. Shanti 320.82
8. Aranyak 33.57
9. जज्ञातेऽर्थविदावुभौ। Adi 57.94
10. स वसतस्तत्रोपाध्यायस्त्रीभिराहूयोक्तः।
उपाध्यायिनी ते ऋतुमती। उपाध्यायश्च प्रोषितः।
—Adi 3.89
11. Aranyak 289-20
12. Adi. 253.6
13. Virat 2.54
14. Aranyak 122.32
15. Ashramvasik 44.50

9

Centres of Learning

The centres of learning during the epic period mostly correspond with the learning centres of the Upnishads period. As centres for higher learning we do not come across any university like Nalanda or Takshashila in the Mahabharata. The centres of learning depicted in the epic can be classified mainly under five heads:

1. Hermitages (Acharyakul or Gurukul)
2. Parishads or Samitis
3. Royal Assemblies
4. Sites of Sacrifice (Yajna Mandapas)
5. Places of Pilgrimage.

We will give a brief account of the above centres of learning as found in the Mahabharata.

1. Hermitages

The most popular term for the main place of learning was "Gurukul" (House of Guru). In the Upnishads, we find the term "Acharyakul" also in place of "Gurugrih" or "Gurukul". In the Mahabharata we find one more substitute, *i.e.* "Gurugrih" for "Gurukul". Generally the preceptor's hermitage was the most popular centre for learning where the students used to have very congenial atmosphere for learning. The Mahabharata tells of numerous hermitages where pupils from distant parts of the country gathered for instruction around some renowned teacher. A full-fledged Ashrama is described as consisting of several departments which are enumerated as follows :

A. Agni-sthan	: Place for fire-worship and prayers.
B. Brahma-sthan	: Department of Veda.
C. Vishnu-sthan	: Department for teaching Raja-Niti, Artha-niti and Varta (comprising Agronomy, Commerce and Public Administration).

D. Mehendra-sthan : Military Section.
E. Vivasvat-sthan : Department of Astronomy.
F. Soma-sthan : Department of Botany.
G. Garud-sthan : Section dealing with Transport and Conveyances.
H. Kartikeya-sthan : Section teaching military organization, how to form patrols, battalions and army.

Dr. R. K. Mookherjee[1] has given a very picturesque description of such two famous hermitages mentioned in the Mahabharata *i.e.* hermitages of Shaunak and Kanva.

The most important of these hermitages was that of the Naimisha, a forest which was like a university. The presiding personality of the place was Shaunaka, to whom was applied the designation of Kulapati, sometimes defined as the preceptor of one hundred thousand disciples. Saunaka attracted to Naimisha a vast concourse of learned men by his performance of a twelve-year sacrifice, of which the most essential part or accompaniment was the discourses and disputations of learned men on religious, philosophical and scientific topics. In one place (Adi 9.37) we read of "ascetics living at Naimisharanya being engaged in a sacrifice lasting for twelve years", on completion of which they set out in large numbers for visiting the various sacred shrines of the country. In another place (Adi 9.14) we have the same reference with the interesting additional information that in the course of that twelve-year sacrifice when a particular one called Visvajit had been completed, the Rishis started for the country of the panchalas and, reaching there, requested the king to give them twentyone strong and healthy calves to be given away as dakshina for the sacrifice they had finished.

Hermitage of Kanva

The hermitage of Kanva was another famous centre of learning, of which a full description is given (i, 70). It is situated on the banks of the Malini, a tributary of the river Sarayu. It was not a solitary hermitage, but an assemblage of numerous hermitages around the central hermitage of Rishi Kanva, the presiding spirit of the settlement. The entire forest was full of hearths where sacred fires burnt, and resounds with the chanting or recitation of sacred texts by learned Brahmins. The wide range and variety of their studies are also indicated. There were specialists in every branch of learning cultivated in that age, specialists in each of the four Vedas, in sacrificial literature and art; Kalpa-Sutras, in the art of reciting the Samhitas according to the Pada and Kramapatha, and Siksha (phonetics), Chhanda (metrics), Sabda (vyakarana), and Nirukta. There were also the philosophers well-versed in Atma-Vijnana (science of the Absolute), in Brahmopasana (worship of Brahma), in Mokshadharma (the way to salvation), and in Lokayata (Vaiseshika). There were also logicians well-versed in the principles of Nyaya, and of Anveekshikee Vidya (Dialectics—the art of establishing propositions, solving doubts and ascertaining conclusions). There were also specialists in the physical sciences and arts, for example, experts in the art of constructing sacrificial altars of various dimensions and shapes (on the basis of a knowledge of Solid Geometry); those who had knowledge of the properties of matter (dravyaguna); of physical processes and their results, of causes and their effects; and zoologists having a special knowledge of monkeys and birds.[2] It was thus a forest university where the study of every available branch of learning was cultivated.

Besides these, there were many hermitages named after the great far-famed scholars like Vyas, Vashishtha, Vishwamitra, Dhaumya, etc. It these hermitages the number of students was quite limited. Maharshi Vyas had only four disciples—Sumantu, Vaishampayan, Jaimini and Pail. In Adi Parvan, there is a description of the hermitage of Dhaumya who had only three disciples—Upmanyu, Aaruni and Veda. Veda is also said to have three disciples. In fact the number of the students was kept limited so that the arrangements for their lodging, boarding, etc., could be made without much difficulty. As a result, it was possible to maintain cordial teacher-taught relationship and treat them as sons. Narad[3] enjoins that the disciples should not be engaged in manual labour and son-like treatment should be given to them.

2. Parishads or Samitis

The existence of a Parishad or Samiti as an agency for educating the people can be traced to as early as the Vedic times. A Parishad was a gathering of learned men including the diplomats and rulers. In the Mahabharata one of the essential qualifications for the membership of a Samiti was that one should be a cultivator also as India was regarded then, and still is, as predominantly an agricultural country. According to F.E. Keay "the Parishads were in some respects like judicial assemblies and in others like ecclesiastical synods, but as most of those who composed them were also teachers, they correspond to a certain extent to the associations of teachers in the Middle Ages of Europe, which developed into universities. Thus not only were different faculties represented, but even a student was a member of the Parishad. The settlement of Brahmans proficient in different branches of the ancient learning in various centres must have meant the gathering together also of a number of students who were receiving instruction from them, and thus these Parishads would form the nucleus of something corresponding to a university".[5]

3. Royal Assemblies

Royal patronage to the scholarship and learning had been one of the salient features of Ancient Indian pedagogic theory and practice. Kings interested in the promulgation of higher learning used to hold tournaments of debate popularly called "Shastrarth". Such tournaments were the best forum for scholars to establish their intellectual position and social status. Rajarishi Janak was the most celebrated patron to such tournaments in which scholars from every nook and corner of the country participated.

In Aranyak Parvan of the Mahabharata it is stated how learned Brahmins were flocking to the sacrifice of Janak "for the purpose of listening to controversies and recitation of the Vedas (Brahmaghosha)". In this very assembly Ashtavakra, son of Kahod and a great exponent of "Monism", got entry with great difficulty as he has only 12 years old and his limbs were affected with certain infirmities. He was very eager to assert and establish his intellectual primacy, but the entrance to the Congress was barred by the gate-keeper who, under the orders of the learned chief named Vandi,[6] was to admit "only old and learned Brahmins". Therefore, firstly, Ashtavakra had to convince the gate-keeper about his eligibility for membership of that learned assembly. Addressing the gate-keeper he asserted, "O gate-keeper, you will today see me engaged in a controversial fight with all the learned men and get the better of Vandi himself in arguments." At the end Ashtavakra claimed victory and his supremacy was acknowledged by the entire assembly. Glimpses of this tournament are found in the Upnishads also. Some contents of the questions are noticed in the Ashtavakra Geeta. The theme of this Geeta is mainly related to self and cosmic soul and various sheds of the relation between the two.

Such Royal Assemblies were important agencies for encouraging and nurturing the higher learning in various branches. The deliberations and disputations of the learned Brahmins on religious, philosophic and scientific topics were very illuminating and inspiring for the participants and other audience too. Elaborate accounts of such assemblies recorded in our Upnishads are milestones in the history of knowledge.

4. Sites of Sacrifices (Yajnya Mandapas)

Hermitages or Gurukulas were permanent seats of learning whereas the sites of sacrifices were quite mobile and of temporary character. The learned gathering which used to be present at various sessions had a great educative significance. These sacrifices were of different durations ranging from one month to twelve years. From Adi Parvan of the epic we learn that, under the supervision of Kulpati Shaunak, one such sacrifice (Vishvajit) was performed in Naimisharanya and lasted for twelve years. Here we find a wonderful gathering of scholars. Vaishampayan had recited the story of the Mahabharata to the various scholars assembled at the sacrifice performed by "Janmejay", son of Parikshit, which was attended by thousands of learned Brahmins. Again it was the sacrifice of Shaunak at Naimisharanya when recitation of the Mahabharata was repeated by Ugrasrava Sauti, son of Lomharshan, renown expert of the Puranas. Thus we can say that "the celebration of these royal sacrifices was the principal agency for the promulgation and popularisation of original literary works of national interest and importance".

5. Places of Pilgrimage

The places of pilgrimage mentioned in the Mahabharata were famous not only for their religious glory but also for their role in disseminating various branches of learning and knowledge in general. These pilgrimages have been associated with our ancient literature like the Vedas, Upnishads, Puranas, etc. Saraswatmuni Tirtha (Shalya, 50.2) is said to be associated with the episode of revival of the Vedas. Due to twelve years of famine the rishis had to desert the bank of the river Sarswati and go elsewhere for their own survival. Because of frequent dislocation they had forgotten the sacred hymns of the Vedas. Under these circumstances they approached Sarswati Muni[7] who was meditating on the Vedas on a solitary bank of the Sarswati and requested him to reteach them the Vedas.

About sixty thousand sages became disciples of Sarswat to study the Vedas. After completing their study they spread out to various places for propagating and reviving the message of the Vedas. In this sages like Sarswat, Apantartama, etc., had a very significant role, references to which are found in a few hymns of the Vedas. But in the Mahabharata we come across detailed accounts regarding the revival of the Vedas. About extinct of Sarswati there are various mythological stories in the Mahabharata. (I, 130-3-4; XI 155.25-27, etc.)

At various places in the epic we find names of several places of pilgrimage. In Shalya Pravan while referring to the pilgrimage of Balram, we find the names of 35 places of pilgrimage, each one of these is related with one episode or the other. The list of 35 places of pilgrimage comprises Prabhas (Shalya, Ch. 34), Gargagotra (Shalya, Ch. 36), Naimishaya Kunj (*Ibid.*), Soma Tirtha, Kuber Thirtha, Kurukshetra, etc. These places of pilgrimage were famous as hermitages also. A list of some such places of pilgrimage are as follows:

1. Kapil Tirtha — Van 81.38
2. Asit — Van 87.9
3. Aashvino Tirth — Van 81.14
4. Kaushik Hrid — Van 82.123
5. Auddalak — Van 82.140
6. Aushan — Van 83.135
7. Gautam Bhavan — Van 82.93
8. Chyvanashram — Van 7.10
9. Dronashrampad — Van 26.26
10. Bhardwajashram — Van 100.5
11. Bharadwaj Tirth — Adi 208.3
12. Matangashram — Van 85.19
13. Markandey Tirth — Van 82.70
14. Medhatithi — Van 212.23
15. Vashisth Parvat — Adi 207.2

In the Mahabharata published by BORI, Pune, we find a list of about four hundred places of pilgrimage. In this very edition we find the narration of episodes also related to the respective places of pilgrimage. Mahamahopaddhyay Kane also in his "History of Dharmashastra" has given one elaborate list of the places of pilgrimage. These places played a vital role in educating the people by inculcating various moral, cultural and spiritual values among the people of the age.[8]

References

1. *Ancient Indian Education,* pp. 333-34
2. ॠचो बव्हृचमुख्यैश्च प्रेर्यमाणाः पदक्रमैः।
शुश्राव मनुजव्याघ्रो विततेष्विह कर्मसु।।
यज्ञविद्याङ्गविभ्दिश्च क्रमद्धिश्च क्रमानपि।
अमितात्मभिः सुनियतैः शुशुभे स तदाश्रमः।।

अथर्ववेदप्रवराः पूगयाज्ञिकसम्मताः ।
संहितामीरयन्ति स्म पदक्रमयुतां तु ते ।।
शब्दसंस्कारसंयुक्तं ब्रुवद्भिश्चापरैर्द्विजैः ।
नादितः स बभौ श्रीमान्ब्रह्मलोक इवाश्रमः ।।
यज्ञसंस्कारविभ्दिश्च क्रमशिक्षाविशारदैः ।
न्यायतत्वार्थविज्ञानसम्पन्नैर्वेदपारगैः ।।
नानावाक्यसमाहारसमवायविशारदैः ।
विशेषकार्यविभ्दिश्च मोक्षधर्मपरायणैः ।।
स्थापनाक्षेपसिध्दान्तपरमार्थज्ञतां गतैः ।
लोकायतिकमुख्यैश्च समन्तादनुनादितम् ।।

—Adi 64. 31-37

3. आचार्यः शिक्षयेदेनं स्वगृहात् दत्तभोजनम् ।
न चान्यत् कारयेत् कर्म पुत्रवच्चैनमाचरेत् ।।

—Narad Smriti 5.16

4. न नः स समितिं गच्छेद् यश्च नो निर्वपेत्कृषिम् ।

—Udyog 36.31

5. F.E. Keay, *A History of Education in India and Pakistan*, p.45
6. Vandi (or Bandi), a court pandit of Mithila, had defeated in argument many great scholars in the past and had them cast into the ocean (Jal-samadhi). Kahod, father of Ashtavakra, was one of those unfortunate scholars. Ashtavakra repaid the debt due to his deceased father by defeating Bandi. Consequently Bandi bowed his head and paid the forfeit by drowning himself in the ocean. Kahod was the disciple and son-in-law of Uddalaka, a contemporary of Yajnyavalkya.

—For details, pl. see Aranyak Parvan, Ch. 132, 133, 134.

7. Shalya 50.44
8. For a detailed study the author's book in Hindi, *Mahabharat Kaleen Shiksha* may be referred, pp.78-91.

10

Teacher-Taught Relationship

The entire gamut of relations between the teacher and the taught (Guru and Shishya) was governed and guided by the common belief that Guru is indispensable and nobody can learn the desired lores (Vidyas) fruitfully without appeasing and satisfying the "Guru". That is why in the Mahabharata it is enjoined that one should never cause enmity with a teacher. He must be kept pleased. In case he is annoyed for some reason or the other, he must be persuaded to be kind and sympathetic to a pupil. One should never condemn or criticize "Guru" as the condemning of the teacher was considered as a burner of one's longevity.[1]

Personal Influence

Nietzsche has rightly emphasized the indispensability of a teacher. According to him, an academic system without personal influence of teachers upon the pupils is an arctic winter. This indispensability of teacher has persistently been emphasised in the Mahabharata and other scriptures.[2] Therefore, students normally developed a sense of reverence and worship towards the "Guru" in and outside their hermitage, during and after the studentship. In certain cases this relationship developed further into father-son relationship. Due to the long stay at the hermitage under the stewardship of the Guru, it was but natural that the relation between the two developed to such an extent. Preceptor's wife and daughter were considered as mother and sister respectively. Matrimonial relation with the preceptor's daughter was prohibited. That is why Kacha refused to marry the daughter (Devayani) of his guru, Shukracharya. Female students were taken as daughters. That is why Arjuna (named Brihannala in disguise) refused to marry Uttara, his pupil in dance and music. However, Arjuna accepted her as his daughter-in-law, *i.e.* as wife of Abimanyu.

Devoted students used to enjoy special favours of the preceptor.

Glory of the student was taken as his own glory by the teacher. He used all his power and exercised all his authority to see that his pupil excelled in the knowledge or lore concerned. Acharya Drona[3] had also taken a vow that he would make Arjuna the best and unparalleled archer. Drona asked Eklavya to present his right-hand thumb in "Guru Dakshina" only because he did not want any rival of Arjuna in archery; Arjuna was dearer to Drona, more dear than his own son.[4] This episode, on the one hand, reveals the weakness of Drona as a teacher and, on the other, his partiality towards Arjuna. At times the teacher-taught relationship was so profound that the preceptors did not hesitate to give their daughters in marriage to their pupils. Acharya Uddalak gave his daughter in marriage to Kahod and Gautam to his pupil Uttank.

Studentship

The preceptor was considered as the spiritual father of the pupil. The following passage (Udyog, Ch. 44) throws good light on the system of studentship and the sacred relationship between the teacher and the taught. It is said that father and mother only create the body; but what the condition derived from the instruction of the preceptor creates is sacred, undecaying and immortal. The preceptor is to be regarded as father and mother and must not be sinned against; because with his grace only the students become masters of learning.[5] The preceptor or Acharya initiate a pupil at the proper time. He lived in close contact with the teacher and as such he was called "Antevasin" (one who lives close to Guru). The teacher-taught relationship was, at times, so profound that the pupils were named after the names of their preceptor such as the disciples of Bhardwaj were called Bhaardwaj. Panini, in his "Ashtaddhyayee", has mentioned two types of students—Dandmanav or Manava and Antevasi. The former denotes the pre-initiation stage and the latter the post-initiation stage when the initiation ceremony has been performed ritually by the Guru. The initiation ceremony (Upnayan Samskar) had a special importance in maintaining a cordial teacher-taught relationship.

Pupils used to lead very dedicated lives in the hermitage. They were everready to perform any job assigned to them by the preceptor. The Guru also looked after them well. One of the famous teachers of Takshashila was Dhaumya, who had three disciples named Upmanyu, Aruni and Veda. Aruni hailed from Panchala and was an ideal student in terms of devotion to his teacher. Once he was ordered by Dhaumya to stop a breach in the water course in his field. Aruni, after having found no other means viable, threw his own body into the breach. His devotion was recognized by his teacher by giving him the appelation of Uddalaka (Uddarak). Yajnyavalkya was the student of Aruni, Shvetketu was Aruni's son. Aruni had earned great fame and glory as a scholar of the Vedas and Vedangas. He had learnt spiritual science from a king named Jaibali Pravahan. His son Shvetketu also followed in his footprints in this regard.[6]

Similarly Dhaumya had tested the devotion of Upmanyu and Veda also. All the three students of Dhaumya stood the test administered by their preceptor successfully and were blessed by him. In the name of guru-sewa (service) some teachers used to compel the students for hard manual work and harass them. Dhaumya used to put Veda even under the plough in place of an ox. Many a student was seriously grieved by such harsh treatment at the hermitage.

Perhaps those students, who were not able to bring adequate money for the preceptor, had to undergo such undesirable trials. But inspite of all suffering and vexing treatment at the hermitage students never took ill of it nor did they have any grudge against the preceptor. The simple reason behind this was their great respect and reverence towards the preceptor.

Later on when Veda[7] himself became a teacher he decided never to make any disciple suffer at his hands. And he had three disciples (Shishyas). But he stood by his decision.

Veda was a famous scholar of the Vedas and Vedangas. Parikshit Janmejey and Paushya had learnt the vedas from him. Uttank was the disciple of Veda. He was an ideal student as far as devotion to the teacher was concerned. The story of Upmanyu[8] confirms the tradition regarding the regulations of the system of studentship. The duties of students included tending the preceptor's cattle, taking care of his field, serving him at the cost of one's life and giving guru-dakshina at the end of the pupilage. Similar details are available in the description of the daily routine of Kacha. In the hermitage as a disciple of Shukracharya (to learn the art of Sanjivini) he (Kacha) performed all the duties to the entire satisfaction of Shukracharya and his daughter, Devayani. After acquiring mastery in the art and use of Sanjivini Kacha once got seriously sick, Shukracharya brought him back to life. He bowed down to Shukracharya and said, "The teacher who imparts knowledge to the ignorant is a father. Besides, as I have issued from your body, you are my mother too." A pupil used to pass his time in the hermitage as one of the members of the preceptor's family. On his part the teacher also made an all-out effort for the all round development of the students under his charge.

Devotion of Uttanka to his Preceptor[9]

The story of Uttanka, like many others, was narrated by Suta Ugrashrava, son of Lomharshan, to the sages assembled in the Naimish forest for a twelve-year sacrifice conducted and monitored by Kulpati Shaunak. While attending the snake-sacrifice of king Janmejaya he listened to the stories of the Mahabharata narrated by Vaishampayana to Janamejaya. The present episode is one of them, which he reproduced in the Naimish forest in the presence of great sages. The story is in prose (except for one verse) and throws light on the teacher-taught relationship in a touching manner.

As we have already mentioned, Dhaumya had three famous disciples. Veda was one of them. Since Veda had suffered a lot at the hands of his Guru, he did not, as said above, want to similarly ill-treat his disciples.[10] Uttanka was the dearest disciple of Veda. Once he put Uttanka incharge of his household and proceeded on some religious assignment. He had instructed Uttanka to do whatever was necessary in the house during his absence. Uttanka took his abode in his preceptor's house carrying out his orders. During his stay here once the ladies of the house called him and told him that his preceptor's wife was in the menstruating period and since the preceptor was out, he should do what the preceptor might have done on such an occasion. Being asked thus, he showed his inability to accede to such an objectionable and unrighteous request.

After some time Veda returned. He was pleased to know all about Uttanka and asked him what good he should do for him. He told Uttanka that he had been served well by him (Uttanka) and hence his affection for him had increased. He showered his blessings on Uttanka and wished for his grand success.

Uttanka, in turn, asked his preceptor what good should he do for him, for, it was said that either of the two—one who best owned knowledge unrighteously and the one who received it unrighteously—would die and enmity would be born between the two. Being told so, the preceptor asked him to stay in his house for some more time. After a few days Uttanka again asked the same question. The preceptor told him that since he had asked the question many times, he should now ask his wife and bring whatever she wanted. Accordingly Uttanka asked the preceptor's wife what she wanted. She asked him to bring ear-rings from the Kshatriya's (wife) or Paushya. She wanted to serve food to the Brahmanas on the fourth day, on the eve of Punyak-vrita, after wearing those rings.

Further she told him that if he accomplished this job, he would be blessed with good fortune.

In order to fulfil the desire of the preceptor's wife he went to Paushya and, after facing many odds and obstacles on the way, he succeeded in getting the ear-rings. When Uttanka gave the ear-rings to the preceptor's wife, she told him that he had arrived in time and marginally escaped her curse. Further she told him that the time of his good fortune had come and he would get success. After that Uttanka went to the preceptor and saluted him. The preceptor asked him the reason for the delay. He explained everything to him. The preceptor then explained the riddle-like things which Uttanka had seen on the way. After this Uttanka took permission from the preceptor and departed for Hastinapur.

This story is found in Aashwamedhik parvan[11] also in a versical form with certain variations. There the preceptor's name is given as Gautam and his wife's name as Ahalya. The moral and ethical values in both the forms are the same, *i.e.* self-restraint, purity, obedience, courteousness and righteousness. The story conveys the message that one should acquire knowledge by serving his preceptor righteously and the preceptor should also instruct the pupil righteously.[12]

Magnanimity of teacher-taught relationship was observed on the battle-field also. When Drona said to Arjuna: "You are returning from the battlefield without conquering your enemy" (Drona himself), Arjuna answered modestly, "You are my preceptor and I am like your son."[13]

Because of the fatherly attitude of the preceptors they did not feel hurt at the rude behaviour of their pupils. When Drona could not complete his vow of catching Yudhishthir alive Duryodhan rudely taunted him : "You are not true to your salt. You depend on us; but look after the welfare of the Pandavas. I was not aware that you are like a honeyed dagger."[14] On this, Drona simply said : "I don't take ill of your words. You are just like Ashvatthama (Drona's son) for me."[15]

There was a specific style[16] of saluting preceptors on the battlefield. By fixing their arrows with the names inscribed on them they used to shoot arrows at the feet of their respective preceptor. The arrows thus shot were to touch the preceptor's feet without hurting them. Thus we see that in side and outside the hermitage, in war or in peace, during and after completion of pupilage the teacher-taught relationship was quite cordial and full of mutual trust and respect. Preceptors treated their pupils as their sons. This very parental attitude is very much lacking now a days on the part of teachers in general.

Eligibility Criteria for Studentship

Manu[17] enjoins that one who is not virtuous, not having any aptitude for service, should not be taught because as a seed sown in a barren land does not yield any produce, similarly a knowledge imparted to the unworthy is of no avail. In the Mahabharata this very idea has been expressed in a personified style. The Goddess of Vidya went to a Brahman and said, "I am your property, please protect me. Do not impart me to any vicious person, then only I will be more effective. Please teach one whom you consider pious, self-restrained and celebrate. Such a person only can be my protector."[18] It was the law that the wise teacher should not refuse a worthy pupil, who sought knowledge of him. So Sukra acceded to the request of Kacha, the grandson of the sage Angira and the son of Brihaspati, and said, "Kacha, you belong to a good family. I accept you as my pupil, the more willingly, that by doing so, I shall also be showing my respect for Brihaspati."

Certain preceptors observed caste restrictions also in imparting the knowledge of weapons or otherwise. Parasuhram, son of Jamdagni, and a great scholar and warrior, was deadly against the Kshatriyas (warrior class). Karna went to Parashuram and became his disciple by representing to him that he was a Brahmana. He learnt of Parasuram the mantra for using the master weapon known as Brahmastra. One day Parashuram was reclining with his head on Karna's thigh. Blood began to flow due to some insect-bite and the pain was terrible, but Karna bore it without a tremor lest he disturb the master's sleep. Parashuram awoke and saw the blood which had flowed from the wound. He said: "Dear pupil, you are not a Brahmana. A Kshatriya alone can remain unmoved under all bodily torments. Tell me the truth."

Karna confessed that he had told a lie in presenting himself as a Brahmana and that he was in fact the son of a Charioteer. Parashuram in his anger pronounced this curse on him : "Since you have deceived your guru, the Brahmsastra you have learnt shall fail you at the fated moment. You will be unable to recall the invocatory mantra when your hour comes."

Guru Dakshina

In the technical sense of the term "Guru-Dakshina" means paying off the debt the pupil owes to his preceptor for his gift of knowledge by suitable presents. Such presents were made in due humility, *i.e.* not thinking at all that he is making a gift to his teacher, much less speaking about it. There are many dignified and subtle episodes interwoven in the Mahabharata which reveal that paying "Guru-Dakshina" was one of the pious duties on the part of the student.

In Adi Parvan and Ashvamedhik Parvan we come across the episode of Uttank, an ideal disciple of Dhaumya.[19] On being asked by wife of Dhaumya, Uttank brought the ear-rings from the queen of the king Sudas. He had to encounter every sort of experience and danger to procure for his preceptor's wife the present of his choice before leaving preceptor's home on completion of his education. From the stories of Uttank, Galav etc. it is obvious that it was based on personal reverence and devotion towards the preceptor and not directed by any religious directive. In this case, the preceptor was not willing to accept any Guru-Dakshina as a token of reverence and respect towards their teacher. In this very waive once Uttank asked his preceptor's wife, "O mother, kindly let me know what should I bring for you, what is dear to you?"[20]

In fact the preceptors were fully satisfied with the righteous conduct and sincere efforts of the pupils for learning different lores.[21] This was an ideal adopted by a section of preceptors. On the insistence of Vartantu his preceptor, Kautsa demanded fourteen crores of gold coins (swarnmudras) as he had learnt fourteen lores from Kautsa. Vartantu got this much amount from the great king Raghu and fulfilled the desire of his Guru.

In the Mahabharata we find the term "Acharya-Vetan" for "Guru Dakshina" which indicates that the ideal was falling from its high pedestal. Acharya Drona had asked his students, Pandava princes, defeat of king Drupad (Drona's classmate) and his kingdom as Acharya-Vetan.[22]

Later on the teachers were classified on the basis of the Dakshina they accepted in return for teaching the Vedas, etc. Such teachers accepting money for livelihood were given the appelation of "Upaddhyay". Acharyas were considered to be superior to Upaddhyayas because the former did not demand money as such for the knowledge they imparted. Manu (2.145) has considered Acharya as ten times more important than Upaddhyay.[23]

Present Deterioration

Nowadays this cordial and harmonious relationship between the teacher and the taught is not visible which is one of the causes of general deterioration in the educational standard. This is partly because of the degeneration in our moral, academic, social, cultural and spiritual values and partly because of the substandard personalities of teachers of the post-independence era. Lack of mutual trust, trust between parent and teacher, teacher and taught, principal and teachers and so on, is also one of the causes of the degeneration of our academic values. These days money has occupied the central place in the entire value system. Every act and conduct, action and reaction is weighed with money. Material prosperity has become the ultimate aim of the teachers almost in all the fields. These days they do not see any wrong in writing cheap help books (guides), doing mass tuitions, helping students in copying in examinations and in adopting foul means, etc.

The teacher-taught relationship in the epic period as compared to the above was far superior and cordial.

Exhortation by the Preceptor

We find in the Taittiriya Upanishad[24] a very interesting passage from several points of view. When the teaching of the Veda is over, the preceptor exhorts the student:

"Speak the truth, Do your duty. Neglect not the daily study of the Veda. After having brought to your teacher his proper reward, do not cut off the line of progeny. Do not swerve from your duty. Do not neglect what is useful. Do not miss opportunities to become great. Do not neglect the daily duties of learning and teaching the Veda. Do not neglect the sacrificial rituals due to the Gods and Fathers. Let your mother be to you like a godess. Let your father be to you like a god. Let your guest be to you like a god. Whatever actions are blameless, those should be followed, not others. Whatever good works have been performed by us, those should be emulated by you, not others. And there are some Brahmanas better than us. They should be comforted by you by giving them a seat. Whatever is given should be given with faith not without it, with joy, with modesty, with politeness and kindness. If there should be any doubt in your mind, with regard to any duty or with regard to conduct, in that case, conduct yourself as Brahmanas, who possess good judgement, conduct themselves therein, whether they be appointed or not, as long as they are not too severe, but devoted to duty. And with regard to things that have been spoken against, conduct yourself as Brahmanas, who possess good judgement, conduct themselves therein, whether they be appointed or not, as long as they are not too severe, but devoted to duty. Thus conduct yourself. This is the rule. This is the teaching. This is the true purport (Upanishad) of the Veda. This is the command. Thus should you observe. Thus should this be observed."

We find an important passage in Charaka[25] Samhita for the medical students:

"When, on getting permission, you begin to practise, you ought to make an effort to offer an adequate honorarium to your teacher. You should aim at the welfare of Brahmanas, cows and all other beings with a view to winning practice, prosperity and fame here and in heaven hereafter. Every day you should continuously and whole-heartedly try to promote the health of patients. Even if your own life is in danger, you should not neglect your patients. You should not entertain an evil thought about the wealth or wives of others. Your dress should be modest and not foppish. Avoid drinking, do not commit a sin, nor help one who is committing it. Your speech should be smooth, polished, truthful and to the point. Taking all facts into consideration, you should make a deliberate endeavour to increase the stock of your knowledge and instruments. Do not give medicine to those whose disease is definitely ascertained to be incurable, or to those who are about to die, or to women, if their husbands or guardians are not present. Do not accept any fees from ladies without the assent of their husbands and guardians. When you enter a patient's room, all your attention should be centred on the patient, his expression, movements and medicines, to the exclusion of everything else. You must treat as strictly confidential all information about the patient and his family. Where there is a danger of the patient or any of his relatives receiving a shock, you should not divulge the impending death of the patient even when you are aware of it. Though well-grounded in our line, you should not praise your knowledge much, for some people get disgusted even with their friends and relatives if they are given to boasting. One can never get a mastery of the entire medical science. Unrelated, one should, therefore, pass one's time in making a constant effort to learn something more. A wise man will indeed gather something from every quarter, a fool only thinks otherwise, and shows jealousy. Taking all things into consideration, a wise physician should listen to and derive benefit from the discoveries or observations even of an enemy, if they are calculated to promote one's fame and prosperity in this world.

The above classical passages include all moral, social and cultural values the preceptors wanted to develop among the students.

Footnotes

1. गुरुणा वैरनिर्बन्धो न कर्त्तव्यः कदाचन।
   अनुमान्यः प्रसाद्यश्च गुरुः क्रुध्दो युधिष्ठिरः।।
   सम्यङ्मिथ्याप्रवृत्तेऽपि वर्तितव्यं गुराविह।
   गुरुनिन्दा दहत्यायुर्मनुष्याणां न संशयः।।

   —Anushasan 107. 46-47

   Compare, Gautam Dharma Sutra, 2-37
2. न बिना गुरुसम्बन्धः ज्ञानस्याधिगमः।

   —Shanti 32.622

   Compare, आचार्याद्धैव विद्या विदिता साधिष्टं प्रापयतीति।

   —Chhandogya 4.9.3
3. प्रयतिष्ये तथा कर्तु यथा नान्यो धनुर्धरः।
   त्वत्समो भविता लोके सत्यमेतत् ब्रवीमि ते।।

   —Adi 123.6
4. यो मे पुत्रात्प्रियतरं सर्वशास्त्रविदुषां वरः ।

   —Adi 125.6
5. आचार्ययोनिमिह ये प्रविश्य भूत्वागर्भे ब्रहमचर्यं चरन्ति।
   इहैव ते शास्त्रकारा भवन्ति विहाय देहं परमंयान्ति शान्तिम्।।
   Compare, आचार्या उपनयमानो ब्रह्मचारिणं कृणुतेगर्भमन्तः।

   —Atharva 11.5.3
6. श्वेतकेतुर्हारुणेय पांचालानां समितिमियाय
   त प्रवाहणो .... भगव इति।

   —Chhandogya 5.3
7. स शिष्यान्न किंचिदुवाच कर्म वा क्रियतां गुरुशुश्रूषा वेति। दुःखाभिज्ञो हि गुरुकुलवासस्य शिष्यान्परिक्लेशेन योजयितुं नेयेष।

   —Adi 3.84
8. Adi. Ch. III
9. Adi Parvan 3.83 to 3.101 and 3.106 to 3. 117
10. Adi 3.84
11. Ashvamedhik Parvan 55.2 to 57.55
12. यश्चाधर्मेण विब्रूयाद् यश्चाधर्मेण पृच्छति।
    तयोरन्यतरः प्रैति विद्वेषञ्वाधिगच्छति।।

    —Adi 3.94
13. गुरुर्भवान्न मे शत्रुः शिष्यः पुत्रसमोऽस्ति ते।

    —Drona 66.33
14. अस्मानेवोपजीवंस्त्वमस्माकं विप्रिये रत।
    न ह्यहं त्वां विजानामि मधुर्दिग्धमिव क्षुरम्।।

    —Drona 69.14

15. नाभ्यसूयामि ते वाचमश्वत्थाम्नासि मे समः।

—Drona 69.14

16. Virat 84. 6.7
17. Manu 2.112-13
18. Udyog 44.9
19. गुर्वर्थं कं पृच्छामि ब्रूहि त्वं द्विजसत्तम।
तमुपाकृत्य गच्छेयमनुज्ञातस्त्वया विभो।।

—Ashvamedhik 55.20

20. आज्ञापयस्व मां मातः कर्त्तव्यं हि प्रियं तव।

—Ashvamedhik

21. दक्षिणा परितोषो वै गुरुणां सभ्दिरुच्यते।

—Ashvamedhik 55.29

22. ततों द्रोणोऽब्रवीभ्दयो वेतनार्थमिदं वचः।
पार्षदो द्रुपदो नाम छात्रवत्यां नरेश्वरः।
तस्यापकृष्य तद्राज्यं मम शीघ्रं प्रदीयताम्।।

—Adi 154. 20-21

23. उपाध्यायान्दशाचार्य —Manu 2.145

24. वेदमनूच्याचार्योऽन्तेवासिनमनुशास्ति। सत्यं वद। धर्मं चर। स्वाध्यायान्मा प्रमदः। आचार्याय प्रियं धनमाहृत्य प्रजातन्तुं मा व्यवच्छेत्सीः। सत्यान्न प्रभदितव्यं। धर्मान्न प्रमदितव्यम्। भूत्यै न प्रमदितव्यम्। स्वाध्यायप्रवचनाभ्यां न प्रमदितव्यम्। देवपितृकार्याभ्यां न प्रमदितव्यम्। मातृदेवो भव। पितृदेवो भव। आचार्यदेवो भव। अतिथिदेवो भव। यान्यनवद्यानि कर्माणि तानि सेवितव्यानि नो इतराणि। यान्यस्माकं सुचरितानि तानि त्वयोपास्यानि नो इतराणि। ये के चास्मच्छ्रेयांसो ब्राह्मणाः तेषां त्वयाऽऽसनेन प्रश्वसितव्यम्।

श्रिया देयम्। ह्रिया देयम्। भिया देयम्। संविदा देयम्। अथ यदि ते कर्मविचिकित्सा वा वृत्तविचिकित्सा स्यात् ते तत्र ब्राह्मणाः संमर्शिनः युक्ता आयुक्ताः अलूक्षा धर्म्मकामाः स्युः यथा ते तत्र वर्तेरन् तथा तत्र वर्तेथाः। अथाभ्यारव्यातेषु ये तत्र ब्राह्मणाः संमर्शिनः युक्ता आयुक्ताः अलूक्षा धर्मकामाः स्युः यथा ते तत्र वर्तेरन् तथा तेषु वर्तेथाः।

एष आदेशः। एष उपदेशः। एषा वेदोपनिषद्। एतदनुशासनम्। एवमुपासितव्यम्। एवम् चैतदुपास्यम्।

—Taittiriya Upanishad 1.11

25. अनुज्ञातेन प्रविचरता (त्वया) पूर्वं गुर्वर्थोपान्वा हरणे यथाशक्ति प्रयतितव्यम्। कर्मसिद्धिमर्थसिद्धिं यशोलाभं प्रेत्य च स्वर्गमिच्छता त्वया गोब्राह्मणादौ कृत्वा सर्वप्राणभृतां शर्माशासितव्यम्। अहरहउत्तिष्ठता चोपविशता च सर्वात्मना चातुराणामारोग्ये प्रयतितव्यम्। जीवहेतोरपि चातुरेभ्यो नाभिदोग्धव्यम्। मनसापि च परस्त्रियो नाभिगमनीयास्तथा च सर्वमेव परस्वम्। निभृतवेशपरिच्छदेन भवितव्यम्।

अशौण्डेनापापेनापापसहायेन व श्लक्षण शुक्ल-धर्म्य-शर्म्य धन्यसत्यहित-मितवचसा देशकालविचारिणा स्मृतिमता ज्ञानोत्थापनकरणसम्पत्सु नित्यं यत्नवता च न कदाचित् .... अनपवाद प्रतिकाराणां मुमूर्षाणां च तथैवासन्निहितेश्वराणां। स्त्रीणामनध्यक्षाणां चौषधमनुविधातव्यम्। न च कदाचित् स्त्रीदत्तमभिदातव्यमननुज्ञातं भर्त्राथवाध्यक्षेण। आतुरकुलं ....चानुप्रविश्य वाङ्मनोबुद्धीन्द्रियाणि न क्वचित्प्राणिघातव्याणि अन्यत्रातुरादातुरोपकारार्थादातुरगतेष्वन्येषु वा भावेषु। न चातुरकुलप्रवृत्तयो बहिर्निश्चारयितव्या। हसितं चायुः प्रमाणमातुरस्य न वर्णयितव्यम् जानतापि तत्र यत्रोच्यमानमातुरस्यान्यस्य वात्युपद्मातात संपद्यते।

—Charak Samhita,
Viman Sthan 8/6-8

11

Masters of Learning (Acharyas)

Great Sage Vyas and His Disciples

In the Mahabharata Vyas is referred to by various names like Krishna Dvaipayan, Dvaipayan, Satyawatisut, Satyawatyatmaja, Parasharya, Parasharatmaja, Badarayan, Ved Vyas. Each of these nomenclatures has some specific semantic connotation reflecting biographical threads and various facets of his personality. He was a historical figure, which has been established now by various traditional evidences and latest Indological researches; but the Western scholars, including W. Hopkins,[1] Keith and Meckdonell[2], Winterneitz,[3] etc., and very few Indian scholars like Hemchandra Raichaudhary[4] opine that Vyas was merely a mythological or legendary figure. It is true that till now we have not been able to pinpoint his date; but this does not and should not reflect upon his historicity. He was an extremely outstanding scholar having unfathomable knowledge and a very firm and dynamic personality. For historical and pauranic knowledge scholars like Vaishampayan and Lomharshan used to revere and depend upon him.[5] He was a great historian. In the very first chapter of Adi Parvan he refers to the great Kings like Rantidev, Valhik, Daman, Shaivya, Sharyati, etc., who contributed a lot to make this land heaven-like and whose glory is still shining in history with imperishable glamour in one way or the other :

येषां दिव्यानि कर्माणि विक्रमस्त्याग एव च।
माहात्म्यमपि चास्तिक्यं सत्यता शौचमार्जवम्।।
विद्वभ्दिः कथ्यते लोके पुराणैः कविसत्तमैः।[6]

By having compiled and classified the Vedas properly he justified his name "Ved Vyas" as such—

विव्यासैकं चतुर्धा यो वेदं वेदविदां वरः।[7]

He had performed a Himalayan task. In this connection, Soot Ugrashrava's remarks are noteworthy:

विविधं संहिताज्ञानं दीपयन्ति मनीषिणः।
व्याख्यातुं कुशलाः केचित् धारयितुं परे।।
तपसा ब्रह्मचर्येण व्यस्य वेदं सनातनम्।
इतिहासमिमं चक्रे पुण्यं सत्यवतीसुतः।।

Vyas was a great Yogi, who could visualize the sequence of events of this land and social history thereof by the virtue of his divine intellectual power and with the help of lord Ganesh recorded the same in the Mahabharata. Regarding his versatile genius the following tribute of Markandeya Puran is very pertinent :

"In this great volume four purusharthas (Dharma, Artha, Kama and Moksha) have been discussed in such a manner that they balance and supplement each other. Its (Mahabharata's) nature of contents is so elaborate that it is competent to be utilized as great Dharmashastra, Comprehensive Arthashastra, leading Kamashastra and a good treatise on Mokshashastra. In this literature of Ved Vyas Mahabharata we come across the code of all the four Ashramas. By following the code of ethics incorporated in this great epic people will be virtuous and useful to the society. Indeed his contemplation was very generous and multi-dimensional.[9]

The Mahabharata is called the fifth Ved. After his name (Krishna) it is also called "Karshna Ved".[10] According to Markandeya Puran he had his hermitage near "Vishala Badri". In this very Badrikashrama Vyas, after the Mahabharata War was over, compiled this grand poetical history in the form of Mahabharata by sustained meditation of three years—

त्रिभिर्वर्षैः सदोत्थायी कृष्णद्वैपायनो मुनिः।
महाभारतमाख्यानं कृतवानिदमुत्तमम्।।[10]

In the "History of Indian Literature," the contribution of Krishna Dwaipayan Vyas is indeed unparalleled.

Vyas taught four Vedas to his four disciples—Sumantu, Jaimini, Pail and Shuka, and the Mahabharata to his son Vaishampayan, who was senior to these four disciples :

प्रभुर्वरिष्ठो वरदो वैशम्पायनमेव च।
संहितास्तै पृथक्त्वेन भारतस्य प्रकाशिताः।।[12]

Thus we see that the Herculean task of compiling and preserving of Vedic hymns contributed by members of various families of sages was performed by Ved Vyas. He also put his best for the integration of Vedic and classical literature, Vedic culture and folk culture. We find very charming glimpses of folk literature in "Yaksha-Yudhishthir Prashna." Similarly, the contribution of his disciples is also remarkable. They have made a landmark in the field of Vedic literature and its various branches. In "Ashwalayan Grihyasutra" in the context of Shradha names of many revered scholars have been referred and Sumantu, Jaimini, Vaishampayan and Pail find a place amongst them. This apparently reflects their standing as great scholars.

Kulpati Shaunak

Shaunak, son of Shunak, belonged to the Bhrigu clan. He was a Kulpati of a great Ashrama located in Naimisharanya. He was a great scholar and ritualist. In the Mahabharata he has been addressed by several names Bhargava, Bhargavottam, Bhrigu Shardul, Bhrigukulodwah, Bhrigunandan, etc. In the field of Brahma Vidya (knowledge of Brahma or Atman) his guru was Angira Rishi. In the Mundakopnishad Shaunak is referred to as approaching Angira with certain queries pertaining to the knowledge of Brahma (Brahma Vidya) :

"शौनको ह वै महाशालोऽङ्गिरसं विधिवत् प्रसन्न पप्रच्छ"[13]

When the serpent-session (sarpasatra) of Parikshit Janmejaya was going on Shaunak was busy in a quite long session lasting for twelve ears at Naimisharanya. After the sarpa-satra was over Soot Ugrashrawa, son of Lomharshan, came down to Naimisharanya, where there was a big gathering of sages[1]. Here Ugrashrawa was informed by the assembled sages that Shaunak was well-versed in stories related to Gods, semi-gods, demons, nagas, etc.:

योऽसौ दिव्याः कथा वेद देवतासुरकथाः ।
मनुष्योरगगन्धर्वकथा वेद च सर्वशः । ।[15]

On this occasion great scholar Shaunak himself expressed his desire to listen the story of the Bhargava clan from Ugrashrawa:

तत्र वंशमहं पूर्व श्रोतुमिच्छामि भार्गवम् ।[16]

This reveals his affection towards his own clan (Bhargava Vansh). When the Pandavas moved to the forest a large number of learned

Brahmins followed them. Shaunak was one of them. Having explained the fashion of working of rational and irrational persons to Yudhishthir Shaunak exhorted him to achieve his cherished goals by practising penances. Shatanik, son of Janmejaya, was also exhorted by Shaunak. Shaunak had also narrated Yayati episode to Shatanik.[17]

Great sage Aashwalayan, expounder of Aitraiya Brahman, was the disciple of Kulpati Shaunak. Shaunak himself subscribed the fifth Aaranyak of the Aaitraiya Aaranyak. According to Bhagvaddatta[18] the following are other shastras of Shaunak:

(1) Aatharvan Shaunak Shakha, (2) Aitraiya Aranyak (V Aaranyak), (3) Kalpa sutra, (4) Rik Pratishakhya, (5) Ten Anukrimani (Table of Contents) of Rigveda, (6) Brihaddevta, (7) Aatharvana Chaturaddhyayee (four chapters), (8) Charana-Vyuha and (9) Rigvidhan.

The above-mentioned works of Shaunak throw a good light on the trends and development of religious literature of that age. Besides the masters of learning (Acharyas) referred in his work authentically indicate the then progress made in the field of literature. The names like Aagastya, Gargya, Panchal, Babhravya, Makshvya, Mandukey, Yaska, Vyadi, Shaktayan, Shakal, Shakalya, Vedmitra, Shakalya Sthvira, etc., mentioned in Rikpratishakhya are indicative of a healthy tradition then prevailing in the field of exchange of ideas. Among these the mention of grammarians like Vyadi, Shakatayan, Gargya, Shakal, etc., indicates regular learning-teaching of Grammar.

Disciples of Shaunak

Aashwalayan and Katyayan were prominent among the disciples of Shaunak. Aashwalayan in his Aaranyak remembers many great scholars—Aitraiyin, Gautam, Kautsa, Sumantu, Jaimini, Vaishampayan, Pail, Shambavya, etc. Reference to Shambavya, writer of Kaushitiki Grihyasutra, reveals that by that time Shambavya had completed his Grihya-sutra. Katyayana was a famous grammarian. According to Yudhishthir Mimansak[19] Vartikas of Vyakaran (critical comments on Sutras of Grammar) were written by Vararuchi, son of Katyayana. Besides being grammarian Katyayan had contributed towards literature on rituals also. Shrauta-sutra, Grihya-sutra, Shulba-sutra, Vajasaneya Pratishakhya, Karma-pradeep, etc., written by Katyayana are available. In his Karma-pradeep[20] there is a reference to Bhishma. In this very treatise[21] he refers to other scholars including Gautam, Shandilya, Shandilyayan, Gobhil, etc. Grihya-sutra of Gobhil is available.

We have already mentioned that the Yayati episode was narrated by Shaunak to Shatanika, son of Janmejaya. Knitted in Adi Parvan of the Mahabharata was narrated gradually by these scholars: Vaishampayana, Janmejaya, Lomaharshana, Shaunak, Shatanika. It appears that the Yayati episode was very popular among the then folk. That is why we come across scholars having expertised in its skilful narration, who were called "Yayata"[22] in the grammatic literature.

Lomaharshana and Ugrashrava

Lomaharshana was the most leading narrator of the Puranas during the Mahabharata period. The very credit of narrating the story of the Mahabharata during the twelve-year session of Kulpati Shaunak at Naimisharanya goes to his son, Ugrashrava. During the serpent-session of Janmejaya, Vaishampayan had narrated the story of the Mahabharata and the same was further elaborated and narrated by Ugrashrava to the great sages and scholars assembled in Naimisharanya. He had personally visited "Samanta Panchak (exact place of battle) and other places of pilgrimage.[23]

In the inceptional period, i.e. prior to Krishna Dwaipayan Vyas, the discourses on the Puranas were undertaken by the people belonging to a particular caste known as "Soot". Later on themes of the Puranas were developed and nourished by Atharva-Angirasas. During this developmental process various themes were interpolated in the Puranas.

Afterwards Vyas infused a lot of innovation and refinement in the Puranshastra. Gradually Purana-vidya was dissociated from the Soot tradition and taken up by sages for its adequate propagation among the people. Lomaharshana, father of Ugrashrava, was a learned Brahmin scholar of this very new tradition, as it is evident from the following statement of Shaunak:

पुराणमखिलं तात पिता तेऽधीतवान्पुरा।
कच्चित्त्वमपि तत्सर्वमधीषे लोमहर्षणे।।[24]

The rishis including Shaunak had heard various divine stories of the Puranas from Lomaharshana also.[25] Since the narration of the Pauranic stories was performed by the persons called "Soot" by caste, these sage-scholars were also called "soot", though they were Brahmins by caste, and as such the word "soot" stood variegated as a mark of profession instead of caste. As the word had traditional inferiority implied in it, in the subsequent period every narrator of the Purana was addressed as "Vyas" in order to provide a sort of elevation to the professionals involved. Similarly, all the Puranas were understood to have been compiled by "Vyas". As a matter of fact various Puranas were compiled in different periods and based on various sectarian cults. Neither these Puranas were compiled at one time nor by the one and the same person. This very fact is proved by the internal evidence also.[26]

Alike Krishna Dwaipayana Vyas his disciple Lomaharshana had also compiled one voluminous Purana, which is said to have four thousand verses.[27] This big Purana of Lomaharshana was the original one. On the basis of this original Puran Akritvrina (named as Kashyap also) and other disciples compiled various Puranas. In the Vayupurana there is a mention of such compilation :

सर्वास्तु चतुष्पादा सर्वाश्चैकार्थवाचकाः ।
पाठान्तरे पृथक्भूता वेदशाखा यथा तथा । ।[28]

Soot Ugrashrawa had studied Puranashastra from his father and from other various scholars as well:

यदधीतं पुरा सम्यग्द्विजश्रेष्ठ महात्मभिः ।
वैशम्पायनविप्राद्यैस्तैश्चापि कथितं पुरा । ।
यदधीतं च पित्रा मे सम्यक्चैव ततो मया ।[29]

The very character of Purana studied by Ugrashrawa from his father is not clear. However, episodes like Aastikakhyan, etc., were taught to him by his father. These episodes only were narrated by him in the Ashrama of Shaunak. We do not find any line of demarcation between Aakhyan and Purana. Actually one Purana contains various episodes and at times for description purpose both were considered as identical, though different in volume. The Mahabharata tells us that traditionally Aakhyan was called Purana.[30]

Maharshi Narada

Narada was a great scholar and very prominent exponent of the cult of devotion (Bhakti path) who has the credit of initiating Prahlad, Dhruva, Ambarish and others in the cult of devotion. He was himself a great devotee of Vishnu. In the Mahabharata[31] he is described as a great scholar of the Vedas and Upnishads, expert in Itihas, Purana, music, grammar Ayurved and other lores.

Narada is regarded as the best, highest and most respected devotee

(Bhakta) of Vishnu. His "Bhakti-Sutra" is very famous, in which Bhakti has been described in the purest manner. Some of the teachings of the Narad Bhakti Sutra are given below

a. After one has established himself in Atma he should continue to preserve and follow the Vedas, and other sacred literature by his activities.[32]
b. Otherwise, there is the probability of his own fall.[33]
c. All moral duties must be properly performed till the body is fit to perform them; although taking of food has to be continued till death.[34]

In Brahma-Vidya Narada's Guru was Sanatkumar.[35] On being asked by Sanatkumar Narad enumerates the various lores he had learnt earlier which include all the four Vedas, Itihas-Purana, fifth Ved (Mahabharata), six Vedangas, logic, Ethics, Astrology, Dhanurvidya, Ayurveda, etc.[36]

Kautilya, in his Arthashastrà, has quoted the opinion of Narada regarding appointment of ministers. Another name of Narad was "Pishun" mentioned in the chapter named "Amatyaniyukti" of Arthashastra. According to Bhagwaddutta[37] 'Pishun' was nick name of Narada. According to Narada the King should have counsel neither from the chief Minister alone nor from all the Ministers; but only the Minister of the concerned portfolio should be consulted in the respective matters. This very counsel quoted in Arthashastra has been reflected in Mahabharata also. On reaching in the assembly of Pandavas alongwith other sages Narada[38] enhances the same type of counsel to Yudhishthir—
All these references reveal that he was a great diplomat also having a very practical outlook.

Great honour is given to Narada because he is said to have revealed to Valmiki the "Ramayana," which opens as follows:

"To sainted Narad, price of those
Whose lore in words of wisdom flows,
Whose constant care and chief delights
Were scripture and ascetic rites,
The good Valmiki, first and best
Of hermit saints, these words addressed
In all the world, I pray thee, who
Is virtuous, heroic, true?
Firm in his vows, of grateful mind,

To every creature good and kind?
Bounteous and holy, just and wise,
Alone most fair to all men's eyes?[39]

Uddhawa

According to the Mahabharata Uddhawa was one of the seven ministers of Vrishni-Andhakas. In the inscription of Yashovarman he has been described as one of the ministers of Andhakas. Another name of Uddhawa, according to scholars like Bhagvaddutta, Yudhishthir Mimansak, etc.,[40] was "Watvyadhi" as he was suffering from rheumatism (gout = Watvyadhi).[41] Kautilya in his Arthashastra has also mentioned the name of "Vatvyadhi" as one of the scholars of earlier times. Taking into consideration the very long association with Andhaka as a minister and long experience of politics, it is reasonable to believe that he must have pondered over various political matters and probably compiled some treatise also on the Arthashastra, which is not available at present; but he has been quoted as one of the famous scholars of the Arthashastra. In the Mahabharata[42] he has been described as an expert in Yoga and Arthashastra.

Bhishma

Sixteenth from Puru, the founder of the Puru branch (Yadu line being its counterpart), came Bharata, from whom India takes its name. Twentythird from Bharat came Shantanu. This Shantanu had two sons—Bhishma from the goddess Ganga (the Ganges) and Vichitravirya by Satyavati. Satyavati had a son named Vyas (from Parashar) before her marriage with Shantanu. Thus Bhishma, Vichitravirya and Vyasa were half-brothers. Bhishma took a vow of celibacy and Vyasa retired to wilderness to live a life of contemplation.

Because of his sober and versatile personality, depth of knowledge and diplomatic talents Bhishma was the most prominent of all characters of the Mahabharata. He was the commander-in-chief of the Kaurava Army for ten days consecutively. At the time when he was seriously wounded and lay on a bed of arrows for 58 days, he exhorted Yudhishthir on various aspects of politics and ethics contained in Shanti Parvan of the Mahabharata. He performed thirty Ashwamedha sacrifices.[43] He was an excellent scholar of the Vedas,[44] and the best among the scholars of Brahma-Vidya.[45] Another name of Bhishma was "Kaunapdanta" (having teeth made of weapon "kunap"[46]). Kautilya in his Arthashastra has quoted the opinion of "Kaunapdanta" in the chapter named "Amatya-niyukti".[47]

In Shanti-Parvan we come across the following three principles regarding the origin of State as propounded by Bhishma :

1. *Social Contract Theory* : In the modern age also philosophers like Rousseau and Locke have propounded this theory. According to this theory for a proper sharing of the people in State affairs the contract between king and subject was considered essential.
2. *Divine Right Theory* : According to this theory king is to be treated as God. Bhishma observed that the king is like God.[48] In the modern age Hobbes is regarded as the propounder of this theory. But there is a substantial difference in the view points of the two. According to Bhishma if the king becomes crooked and malevolent his deeds should be opposed but Hobbes holds a different opinion. According to him any revolt against the king is neither just nor legal, whereas Bhishma enjoins even assassination of the king, who deviates from the path of his duties and proves to be a source of torture to his subjects. He says :

   अरक्षितारं हर्तारं विलोप्तारमदायकम्।
   तं स्म रजकलिं हन्युः प्रजा संभूय निर्घुणम्।।

3. *Organic Nature of the State* : According to Bhishma there are seven parts of a state: king, minister, territory, fort, treasury, military and allies (friendly States).[50] The scholars like Manu, Kautilya, Shukracharya have also referred to these seven parts with a slight variation in names. Comparing these to parts of human body Shukraniti[51] maintains that king is like head, minister is like eye, friends are like ears, treasury is like mouth, military power is like mind, fort is like hand whereas territory is like legs.

In Shanti and Anushashan parvans we come across quite an elaborate exhortation in the form of discourses addressed to Yudhishthir. He left no aspect of life untouched during his elaborate discourses which continued for about two months (58 days). Here we will try to summarize his selected maxims on various values having a bearing on education in its broader sense.

Parents and Teachers

The parents and teachers are three worlds (Trailokya). One conquers this world by doing service to the father, the upper world by doing service to the mother and the Brahma Loka by doing service to the teacher. A teacher is greater than the parents in one way : the parents create the body, while the teachings of guru know no old age.

Three Enemies of a Person

Bhishma referred to certain strong enemies of a man which cause him endless miseries. "A person who is not cautious is caught napping by these enemies, which are always awake and in search of victims. One of them is anger which is born of greed and can be subdued by patience. Another is desire born out of thought and can be eliminated by non-attachment. Ignorance induces a person to commit sins and a person can remove his ignorance by the company of learned people.

Highest Knowledge

Brahmajnana is the highest knowledge; it is eternal. It is Maya which enslaves a person and he finds it difficult to perceive the Parmatman which is within him only. One can gain salvation through all three means Karma, Bhakti and Jnana.

Self-control

Time passes and the man who grows older finds his hair, teeth and eyes grow older. The only things that never grow old are thirst for riches and love of gold.

This is the sum of all righteousness: Treat others as you would like to be treated.

Before decay weakens your body and the ender breaks up your fragile body, lay up the only treasure: Do good deeds and amass that wealth.

Heaven's gate is very narrow and minute. Foolish people, blinded by attraction of the world, fail to see it. Its portals are closed with bolts of pride, passion, avarice and lust.

True Friend

Man is born alone and dies alone. He has no other companion in his journey. Only dharma follows him.

Dronacharya

Drona was a great scholar of the Vedas and a renowned warrior. He was married to Kripi, a sister of Kripacharya.[52] From her he got a brave son named Ashwatthama.[53] Alike Bhishma, Drona was very famous in warcraft. It shows that caste had not yet completely formed itself, Kshatriyas had not yet obtained the monopoly of the use of arms, nor Brahmans of religious learning. Insulted by one of his class-mates, Drupada, the King of Panchalas, he (Drona) retired in disgust to the court of the Kurus and undertook to train the princes in arms. Having trained the princes in the art of using various arms he demanded the customary reward for his tuition (Guru Dakshina). Like the doughty warriors of the old he held revenge to be the dearest joy of a warrior, and for his reward he asked the help of the Kurus to revenge on Drupada, who had insulted him. The demand could not be refused. Drona marched against Drupada, conquered him, and wrested half his kingdom.

In the epic battle Drona fought on the Kaurava side and Drupad, being the father-in-law of the Pandavas, favoured them. Drona, with his impenetrable phalanxes, killed his old rival Drupad.

Dronacharya, second Commander-in Chief of the Kaurava army, was also killed. Furious over this, Drona's son Ashwatthama killed Pridyumna and his other inmates unfairly when they were fast asleep in their camp.

Drona, great exponent of archery and preceptor of Kuru and Pandu princes, is called Drona Bhardwaj. Bhardwaj is, in fact, a paternal names attributed to all the sons, descendants and disciples of Bhardwaj. In ancient Hindu literature there are reference to many Bhardwaj, i.e. Sukesha Bhardwaj.[54] Gardabhavipit Bhardwaj,[55] Krishna Bhardwaj[56] and Drona Bhardwaj.[57]

Amongst these, the last one is known as Dronacharya. In the Arthashastra[58] there are a few opinions quoted in the name of Bhardwaj, which are of Dronacharya only as per the commentators of the Arthashastra. In Drona Parvan he himself claims to have studied Arthashastra (political science) along with the Vedas and their six Angas.[59] He had been an ideal for archerers[60] and a replica of Brihaspati and Shukracharya[61] as far as scholarship in Dandniti was concerned.

Shukracharya

A great scholar of Dandniti, Yoga and medicine, Shukracharya, son of

Bhrigu, has been described mainly as the priest and preceptor of demons, by whose power dead demons were restored to life. Another name of Shukra was "Ushanas Kvya". In the Mahabharata (Bhagavadgeeta) Krishna describing his own divine qualities says:

मुनीनामप्यहं व्यासः कवीनामुशना कविः[62] ।

[I am Shukra (Ushana) among the sages]

Demons later on were called Asuras. Initially the word Asura was used for gods. In fact Deva (god) and Asura were synonymous expressions in a multitude of texts. In one of his articles Dr. Banerjea[63] suggests reconciling of these contradictory uses of the term "asura". Before the Indo-Aryans arrived in India they lived in close proximity to the Persians, the original worshipers of fire. According to him, "What could be more natural than that the Asura-Prachetas, or Asura-Vishaveda was but the translation of the Ahur-Mazda (the wise lord according to the Zend-Avesta) of the other branch and that the word "Ahur", which the one used in divine sense, would become a household word in the other branch in the same sense". Later on the word "Ahura" was changed into "Asura", which was used in Assyria for the Supreme Lord. For some time Assyrians were rulers of the Persians. Therefore, the Kings of Assyria and Persia as well used to pay high regards to Shukracharya. On the Zend-Avesta we find influence of Shukracharya. He is described as subscriber of many hymns known as "Atharvan sukta". He was revered among gods and demons as well.[64] He was contemporary of Yayati (son of Nahush) and Vrisparva (king of demons). His daughter Devyani was married to Yayati, a famous king of his time.

He was a great exponent of the Arthashastra which was termed as Dand Niti also. According to Dr. Jayaswal, "Dand Niti" was the title adopted by Ushnas and Arthashastra by Brihaspati for their respective works, which were very famous in "Hindu classical times".[65] The work famous as "Shukra Niti" is said to be the work of a later time by some other scholar. It is quite possible that as a token of his reverence towards Shukracharya, he must have named it as "Shukra Niti".[66]

Mahamati Vidur

Vichitravirya, son of Satyavati and Shantanu, died childless. Therefore, Satyavati asked her son Vyas (from Muni Prashar) to marry the childless widows. Vyas obeyed. As a result Dhritrashtra was born from Ambika and Pandu from Ambalika. Dhritrashtra was blind by birth whereas Pandu was born with a pale complexion for certain psychic complexes of their mothers during the time of conception. Not being satisfied with these children Satyawati wished for another and perfect child. But Ambika, unwilling herself' dressed up one of her maidservants (Dasis) and sent her to Vyas in her steed. Consequent upon this the Dasi gave birth to a male child, who was called Vidur. After fulfilling his mother's command, Vyas returned to his ascetic life.[67] In course of time Vidur became very eminent for his virtue and wisdom, though he could not be king as his mother was a Shudra.

As far as his talents, wisdom and scholarship are concerned, he is said to have excelled even Brihaspati, preceptor of gods and Shukracharya, preceptor of demons (asuras):

बृहस्पतिर्वा देवेषु शुक्रो वाऽप्यसुरेषु च।
न तथा बुद्धिसम्पन्नो तथा स पुरुषर्षभ।।[68]

He was well-versed in various languages. When he smelt the conspiracy of Duryodhan against the Pandavas to be carried out at Lakshagriha he had advised Yudhishthir in Mlechha Bhasha.

In Udyog Parvan of the Mahabharata there is a up-parvan styled as Prajgar Parvan, in which there are eight chapters and five hundred and thirty verses. In the ethical literature, being separately published, it is known as "Vidur Niti".[69] These verses are in the form of advice given to Dhritrashtra on his request when one night he suffered severely with insomnia. "Vidur Niti", which has made a mark in the ethical literature, runs from Ch.33 to 40 of Udyog Parvan. There is a very subtle explanation of various moral, social and spiritual values like truth, non-violence, non-stealing, purity, austerity, devotion to God, self-discipline, piety, forgiveness, righteousness, freedom from hypocrisy, charity, sincerity, etc. Dr. V. S. Agrawala[70] calls this advice as "Prajnya Shastra" (science of reasoning). Linguistically "panda" is the corrupt form of "prajnya" only and the one who possesses this is called "Pandit" as it has been defined in the Vidur Niti.[71]

Footnotes

1. *The Great Epic of India*, p. 58.
2. *Vedic Index* (1912), p. 339.
3. *Indian Literature*, p. 324.
4. *Political History of India* (V Edn. 1950), pp. 1-57.

5. Vayu Puran 1. 23-25.
6. Adi 1. 181-182.
7. *Ibid.*, 5.45.
8. *Ibid.*, 1. 51-52.
9. Markandeya Puran 1.6-7.
10. Adi 99.15.
11. *Ibid.*, 56.32.
12. *Ibid.*, 57.75.
13. Mundakopnishad 1.1.3.
14. Adi 1.1-3; 4.1.
15. *Ibid.*, 4.4.
16. *Ibid.*, 5.3.
17. Matsya Puran 25.3.
18. भगवद्दत्तः भारतवर्ष का वृहद् इतिहास (भूमिकात्मक), पृ. २९९.
19. व्याकरणशास्त्र का इतिहास, पृ. २१२.
20. भीष्मस्य ददतः पिण्डान्। Karm Pradeep 3.10.9.
21. Karm Pradeep 2.7.21.
22. Kashika-Sutra 6.2.103.
23. Adi 8.1-11.
24. Adi 5.1.
25. *Ibid.*, 5.2.
26. पुराणसंहिताश्चक्रुः बहुला परमर्षयः। Markandeya 45.21.
27. Brihmand Puran 1.35, 63-69.
28. Vayu Puran 61.59
29. Adi Parvan 5.4
30. इतिहासमिमं वृद्धा पुराण परिचक्षते। Adi 13.6.
31. Sabha Parvan, Ch.V.
32. भवतु निश्चयं दाढ्यादूर्ध्व शास्त्ररक्षणम्। Narda Bhakti Sutra 12.
33. अन्यथा पतत्याशंकया। Sutra 13.
34. लोकोऽपि तावदेव भोजनादि व्यापारस्त्वा शरीरधारणावधि। Sutra 14.
35. Chhandogya 7.1.3.
36. *Ibid.*, 7.1.2.
37. *Bhartiya Sanskriti Ka Itihas*, p. 26.
38. कच्चिन्मन्त्रयसे नैकः कच्चिन्न बहुभिः सह। Sabha 5.19.
39. Griffith's *Ramayana*, 1.3.
40. भारतवर्ष का बृहद् इतिहास, भाग–२ (संवत् २०१७) पृ. २१९.
41. कवि स्रमचन्दकृत आयुर्वेदशास्त्र का इतिहास, भाग–१, पृ. ११५.
42. निविष्टास्तान्निशम्याथ समुद्रान्ते स योगवित्।।
    जगामामन्त्रय तान्वीरानुद्धवोऽर्थविशारदः।। Mausal Parvan 4.10.
43. Bhishma Parvan 22.15.
44. Shanti Parvan 122.47.
45. ब्रह्मविदां श्रेष्ठः। Bhishma 115.12.
46. Trikand Kosh 2-8.12

47. नेति कौणपदन्तः। Arth Shastra 1.3.7.
48. Shanti 65.291.
49. Shanti 57.27.

 cf. मोहाद्राजा स्वराष्ट्रं य कर्षत्यनवेक्षया।
 सोऽचिरात् भ्रश्यते राज्याज्जीविताच्च।।

 Manu 7.111

50. Shanti 60.19.
51. Shukra Niti 1.61.
52. Adi 121.11.
53. *Ibid.*, 121.14.
54. Prashnopnishad 6.1.
55. Brihadaranyakopnishad 4.1.5.
56. Kashyap Samhita Sutra 27.3.
57. Adi 121. 6-7.
58. Artha Shashtra 1.3.7 infra
59. वेदं षडङ्गं; वेदाहमर्थविद्यां च मानवीम्। Drona 5.19.
60. विद्यां यस्योपजीवन्ति सर्वलोकधनुर्भृतः। Drona 8.21.
61. बृहस्पत्युशनस्तुल्यो बुद्धया। Drona 8.14.
62. Bhishma Parvan 32.37.
63. Bengal Magazine, April 1880.
64. योगाचार्यो महाबुद्धिर्दैत्यानामभवद्गुरुः।
 सुराणां चापि मेधावी ब्रह्मचारी यतव्रतः।।

 Adi. 48.5

65. *Hindu Polity* (1967), p. 5.
66. Dr. Shyam Lal Pandey, *Bharitya Rajyashashtra ke Praneta*, p. 42-43.
67. Adi Parvan ch.101.
68. Ashram Vasik Parvan 35.13.
69. Publsihed with Hindi translation by Geeta Press, Gorakhpur.
70. *Bharat Savitri* (Hindi), Part 2.
71. यस्य संसारिणी प्रज्ञा धर्मार्थावनुवर्तते।
 कामादर्थं वृणीते यः स वै पण्डित उच्यते।।

 Udyog 33.25

12

End Note

The Mahabharata presents the picture of the society with descending social order with certain fibres of social degeneration and deterioration. The system of education is, of course, a sub-system of the entire social system. Therefore, the over-all picture of the educational system also sounds deteriorating accent. The freedom and opportunity for higher learning available to women-folk during the Vedic time are not visible in the Mahabharata. Moreover, being a feudal society education was largely restricted to the priestly class. Education was mostly available to the members of the royal family or to the affluent. It was the princely and noble families only that the children used to have the privilege of special tutors to teach them at home. Otherwise students had to go to the hermitages in the far-flung forest areas, where the safety problem generally persisted. Because of this the women-folk were not sent to these hermitages for their education. Therefore, they had their education at home itself by the elderly persons of the family or the guest visitors.

So far as the aim of education was concerned it was not confined to the three R's. A multi-dimensional curriculum was available for higher learning which included training in the arms to the training in the science of medicine and surgery; different occupations and vocations also formed part of the curriculum to prepare useful and refined citizens for the society by inculcating in them various moral, social, cultural and spiritual values. Infusion of piety, righteousness, formation of character, development of personality, inculcation of civic and social duties, promotion of social efficiencies and preservation of national culture may be found prescribed as some of the objectives of the educational system depicted in the epic.

The system of education as a whole was more informal than formal, because there were no fixed hours for teaching-learning nor were there definite prescribed text-books. It was only verbal communication between the teacher and the taught. Methods and modes of teaching also differed from person to person and place to place. There was no symmetry or harmony in the various methods of teaching applied at various places. Study of the Vedas, Vedangas, Political Science, Trade and Commerce—these were the main branches of learning. Besides these, the study of various positive sciences like Materia Medica, Chemistry, Botany, etc., were also taught. Special training in arms and in physical fitness was provided to the princes. Education in military science was the nucleus of the entire system of education.

Varnas and Ashramas were the two most important social institutions. The students received their education at Gurukuls during the period of celibacy, received i.e. the first Ashrama. After attaining knowledge and taking permission of the preceptor, they used to return home to become house-holders. The number of students in a Gurukul was limited, and as such there was no problem of discipline. The knowledge and skills acquired by the students were tested through different informal tools and techniques. At times sacrifice, modesty, obedience and other virtues were also tested by the respective preceptors. The women-folk were provided good training in fine arts at their homes wherever facilities existed.

Teaching was mainly the job of Brahmins. But in the area of knowledge, no differentiation was made on the basis of caste or creed. Therefore, in the epic we find examples of many low-descended commanding prestige and reputation in society on the basis of their distinguished achievement in the field of knowledge as well as their personal conduct and attitude towards their mission and not by the virtue of their being simply Brahmins. Brahminhood was not the condition for commanding honour and reputation in society. In the epic we find good many examples of poor Brahmins who had to lead a life in distress and hardship. The teacher-taught relationship was just like between father and son. The students stayed at the hermitages like members of the family of the preceptor. Thus, they were influenced by the grand and noble personalities of the preceptors. This very impact of the guru went a long way in shaping their personality. But unfortunately this very impact or influence is greatly lacking these days. Teachers nowadays do impart knowledge but they are not able to influence the pupils under their charge. This was not the case during the epic time.

Vital Role in National Integration

Royal patronage was one of the most powerful sources for the propagation of knowledge. That is why the system of education even though informal in character was very impressive and fruitful. As centres of learning we find mention of five types, i.e. hermitage (Gurukul), parishad or samiti, royal assemblies, sites of sacrifices (yajnya mandapas) and places of pilgrimage. Among the hermitages, the hermitage of Kulpati Shaunak (Naimish) and of Kanva were most renowned centres of learning wherein the scholars flocked from various corners of the country in the quest of knowledge. The places of pilgrimage played a very important role in the propagation of knowledge and various socio-religious traditions. They also played a very vital role in bringing about national integration and propagating Indian culture abroad.

In this system of education we see a most influential picture of the society prevailing during that time. The basic concept on which the cordial teacher-taught relationship was based was the concept of indispensability of teacher in the process of education. That is why the relation between the pupil and the teacher was very harmonious and cordial. They were united by mutual confidence, respect and affection, though at times a few teachers behaved in a very vexing tone.

The most interesting character of the educational system was that there was no fixed place of learning or teaching. Even the discussion on subtle topics like the self and the supreme can be visualized at a marketplace, in a butchery or at the shop of the grocer. This is only indicative of the fact that pomp and show was not favoured at all in the field of education. Simple living and high thinking was the order of the day.

The essence of education lies in the moral or religious education depicted in the epic. We find very critical analyses of our moral and social values interwoven in the various episodes. At times we find contradictory statements regarding various moral values. But if we go deep into the philosophy of the values, we come to the conclusion that the viewpoint of the Mahabharata has been very practical and appealing. The epic obviously holds that our various moral and social values are subject to change from time to time and from place to place. Therefore, we find the mention of two sets of principles, which can easily be called as Yug-dharma and Sanatan-dharma. The former stands for the changeable set of values while the latter for the eternal set of values. We also find mention of various negative values. At places it has been advised that an individual must also know the nature of the negative values so that he may not be adversely affected by them.

Due respect was given to the low-ascended person if they were found to be of good moral character or very high wisdom. Due respect was also given to the shudras in society. In the field of education we find many low-descended persons enjoying high prestige in society by the virtue of their learning and wisdom. Mahamati Vidur was one of such individuals who commanded great respect in and outside the palace of the Pandavas. "Vidur Niti" is a part of the Mahabharata like the Bhagavadgita. The former is the elaboration of the sermons given by Vidur to Dhritrashtra and the latter is the exhortation of Lord Krishna to Arjuna when he was quite perplexed and frustrated on the battlefield. Similarly from the charioteer class Sanjay and Loharshana enjoyed honour and respect in the royal family. The contribution of the warrior class towards the propagation of spiritual knowledge need not be over emphasized. There were many scholar kings who patronized learning to the best of their ability. The detailed account of the royal patronage by such warrior class to the spiritual knowledge is documented in the Chhandogya Upanishad. Janak was one of the most celebrated patronizer of spiritual knowledge. He was himself a great scholar of Yoga and other allied scriptures. But he mainly believed in rationalism.

Besides the scholar-king we find a galaxy of great scholars in the Mahabharata who contributed substantially towards the propagation of various branches of learning. Among these are the sage Vyasa and his disciples, Kulpati Shaunak, disciples of Shaunak, Lomaharshana and Ugrashrava, Maharshi Narada, Uddhava, Bhishma, Dronacharya, Shuracharya, Mahamati Vidur, Kahod, Uddalak, Shwetketu, Ashtavakra, Chyavan, Bharadwaj, Vishwamitra, Kapil, Asit, etc.

The priest class occupied a very prominent and respected place in the field of learning and knowledge. However, because of their paramount supremacy, later on, they had to face opposition by the warrior class. Various stories of struggle between the warrior class and the priest class for supremacy in the field of knowledge are depicted at various places in the epic.

Relevant Even Today

From the critical survey of various educational ideals and institutions depicted in the epic we come to the conclusion that it was a system of education national in character and appealing to the masses. The principles and theories propounded during the epic period are relevant even today with certain modifications and innovations.

Appendix I

STORIES FROM MAHABHARATA (Based on Spiritual and Cultural Values)

Bhrigu and Varuna*

Bhrigu was one of the eight mind-born sons (Manasputras) of Brahma (In the epic only seven are mentioned). Bhrigu is said to be one of the composers of hymns and narrators of the Mahabharata. Bhrigus are also described as discoverers of fire. From education point of view this story has special significance. It reveals that apart from other ingredients, parental care was considered quite important for the mental growth and guidance of the child. Bhrigu learnt the knowledge of the supreme from his father Varun. But, how patient the father had to be to impart this knowledge can only be understood from the following story.

Bhrigu, the son of Varuna, went to his father and asked for knowledge about the Brahman. The father pointed out that matter, the vital air, the eyes, the ears, the mind and speech were the things one came across in one's experience, but what one should actually try to find is the real Entity from which all these came, towards which all these moved and in which all these finally merge. Varuna's further said that Reality was the Brahman and that it could be known or comprehended only through tapas or meditative austierities. He, therefore, commended to his son the performance of tapas in order to realize the Brahman.

The son started his tapas accordingly. After he had been engaged in it for some time it struck him that the gross matter itself was the Brahman as it was in matter that all beings took their birth, and in matter it was that these finally merged. He went to his father with this conclusion and asked him whether his discovery was correct. Not agreeing with the son's finding, the father asked him to do penance again and realize the truth.

Bhrigu obeyed. This time he felt that the vital air was the Brahman

---

* Bhishma, Ch.32; Rigveda I 58.6, 127.6 143.4; Anu, Ch. 25, Manu 5.1, 5.3.

and found that all his former reasoning applied to this new discovery also. He went again to his father and laid before him the fresh discovery. The father again did not agree and asked his son to undertake a further course of penance in order to know the real truth.

Bhrigu again started his austerities for the third time. After some time is occurred to him that it was the mind which was the Brahman. His former arguments now appeared to him to apply with greater force to mind rather than to either gross matter or to vital air. He went again to his father with this new discovery and wondered whether this time he was correct. Still the father would not accept the son's finding and the later was asked to do penance once again and seek out the truth.

After a further course of penance Bhrigu thought that knowledge or one's power of understanding was the real Brahman. It appeared to him that this finding satisfied the needs of his father's arguings. He, therefore, approached his father and apprised the latter of the latest discovery. Varuna was still unmoved and so Bhrigu had to go again and continue his tapas. Finally, he had the revelation that it was bliss (or Ananda) that was the real Brahman. It was clear to him now that all beings took their origin in bliss, moved towards that bliss and finally coalesced in bliss. When, this time he placed his finding before his father, the latter was overwhelmed with joy at his son having at last found for himself the real truth about the Brahman. Confirming the correctness of the son's finding after a patient waiting and long courses of penance, the father offered the following as his further explanation of the truth:

> Bliss is indeed the highest state of existence. All these five things, viz. matter, vital air, mind, knowledge and bliss, are the five sheaths, as it were, the one being more subtle than that preceding it. Thus bliss is the subtlest of all the five sheaths. None of these sheathes is to be taken as being exclusive of the others. All these are really inter-penetrating. The basis of all these is, however, bliss, which is unalloyed pure happiness and is the Brahman.

Appendix II

NARADA AND SANATKUMARA*

The dialogue knitted in to the Chhandogya Upnishad between Narada and Sanatkumara throws good light on teacher-taught relationship as well as on the significance of the Brhmavidya (knowledge of the Supreme). Narada is also described as an eloquent messenger of the Gods, either to one another or to the favoured mortal. Because of this very quality he is named as "Pishun", also in Kautilya's Arthashastra. In modern plays he is introduced as a spy or marplot. The name Narada is frequently employed as a term of abuse. It is used to describe a quarrelsome, meddling person.

The great sage Sanatkumara of the Vedic days was once asked by Narada, a seeker after truth, about the the real path towards knowledge of the Supreme. Before undertaking to enlighten the questioner on the subject Sanatkumar desired to know how much Narada had already learnt. When asked to state that, Narada unfolded a long list of the texts over which he had acquired mastery. His inventory of these texts included the following: The four Vedas, Rig, Yajus, Sama and Atharva; the Epics and the Puranas; the details of performance of the Shraddha ceremony; grammar (Vyakarana); philology, mathematics, astronomy, astrology, magic, logic, philosophy, knowledge about the various Gods of heaven and their powers, knowledge of animal life and of warfare. After reciting this long and impressive list, Narada, however, confessed to a feeling that, in spite of all that learning, he did not have the essence of knowledge. Then followed between the two the following conversation :

Sanatkumara: you are right in thinking so, Narada. What all you have mentioned is a series of mere names and nothing else.

Narada: Then, Sir, which is it that is greater than mere words and names?

Sanatkumara: Speech is grater than words, because, without speech, there would be no words, or, for that matter, not even any Vedas, nor truth nor religion.

---

* Sabha, Ch. 5; Chhandogya 7.1; Bhagwat Skandha I, Ch. 6; Ramayan Ayodhya, Ch. 100; Narad Samhita Shanti, Ch. 38, 327

Narada: Could you mention anything that is greater than this power of speech, Sir?

Sanatkumara: Yes, mind is greater than speech, because, without the thinking of the mind, there could be neither speech nor words.

Narada: Anything greater than the mind, Sir?

Sanatkumara: The will is greater than the mind, because, it is the will that makes the mind think.

Narada: Is there anything that is greater than the will, venerable Sir?

Sanatkumara: Yes, there is a thing called consciousness which is greater than will. Unless one is "conscious" of a thing, one cannot make one's will start moving by making the mind think.

Narada: Anything greater than consciousness, Sir?

Sanatkumara: Meditation is greater than consciousness, because it is meditation alone that makes things stand firm and steady.

Narada: Kindly tell me, Sir, if there is anything greater than meditation.

Sanatkumara: Power of understanding being sine qua non for proper meditation, that is greater than meditation. If we cannot correctly understand and discriminate between good and bad, truth and untruth, and the like pairs of opposites, how can we meditate?

Narada: If there is still a greater thing than this power of understanding, please let me know what it is.

Sanatkumara: Physical power is certainly greater than all these, because there is nothing like mainly valour when it comes to a question of inspiring awe into others. One strong and physically powerful person is greater than a multitude of imbeciles.

Narada: Is there anything, Sir, which surpasses even physical power?

Sanatkumara: Yes. Food is greater than physical power. This should be obvious to you from the fact that a man starved for a few days will start losing his physical energy and power and may eventually even die. Such a famished person, given food again, will get all his former physical power restored.

Narada: Surely, Sir, there is something which is greater than even food. What is it?

Sanatkumara: Water is greater than food, because without it there will be no food.

Narada: Anything greater than water, Sir?

Sanatkumara: "Heat is greater than water. It is heat that makes the waters of the earth get converted into vapour and form clouds which give rain to the universe."

Narada: Kindly tell me, Sir, if there is anything greater than heat.

Sanatkumara: The ether or akasa is greater than heat. It is in ether that we find the sun, the moon and the stars and it is again in ether that the sound waves traverse.

Narada: I wonder, Sir, whether there is anything which is greater than even this ether. If there is any such, do kindly tell me about it.

This last question of Narada brought the sage's teaching to its climax. Starting with the statement that the Atman or the Supreme Spirit is greater than everything else he expounded about this ultimate Reality in the following words:

It is the joy of doing a thing that makes a man do it. That joy is unlimited. That limitless infinity is the Atman. It is all-pervading. He who realizes the Atman enjoys perfect bliss or happiness. This realization can come only to a mind which is pure. This purity of mind results from pure food. Truth can be contemplated upon only by a pure mind.

The above teaching of Sanatkumara to Narada is called *para vidya* or realization of the Eternal Spirit which confers on the person knowing it deathlessness and everlasting joy.

UDDHALAKA ARUNI*

The actual name of Uddhalaka, great expounder of Brhmavidya, was Aruni Panchal, being the son of Arun. Uddalak was one of the capable disciples of Ayod-dhaumya. He was very much devoted to his preceptor. The name Uddalaka was given by Ayod-dhaumya because he once protected from flooding the field of the preceptor by closing the breach in the water course by laying down his own body after every other means had failed.

When young Svetaketu came of age, his father, Uddhalaka Aruni asked him to go to a preceptor, practise brahmacharya (or celibacy) under him and learn the sacred texts with his guidance. Such type of life, in vogue in the days of the Upnishads, was known as Gurukulavasa.

The son went to a guru accordingly, spent the prescribed twelve years in his hermitage and, after the completion of his learning in the traditional manner, returned home. The father saw that the son was puffed up with pride about his studies and did not possess that serenity of mind which along is the index of true learning. Uddhalaka was, therefore, sure in his mind that his son, Svetaketu, had missed the essence of the teaching for which the latter had been sent out for gurukulavasa.

The father then started testing his son's knowledge. He asked him whether he had learnt about that particular knowledge which enables one to know the great unknown. The very question made Svetaketu feel that his learning had been incomplete and perfunctory. Rather than attempt an answer and plead ignorance he thought it wise to request his own father to impart that knowledge to him. Then the father began his exposition as under:

> Many things are made out of clay, such as pots, toys and the like. The essential thing that one should know about these is the knowledge of the basic component, clay. The rest are all mere forms and names.
>
> Likewise, out of steel are made objects such as the sword, the razor blade, the knife, and the needle. But once the basic metal

* Aranyak Parvan, 132. 1-9, Satpath, 11.4.1, Aadi, Ch.120.

> of steel itself is known, all these various forms and names of that metal are also known.
>
> Thus what matters is the knowledge of the essence of things, which forms the basis of the vast multitudes of names and forms in this Universe.
>
> There was, in the beginning, one and only Being—One without a second. That Being desired to become many. Thus came forth the Universe with its myriads of things, finally with life and man himself as the highest embodiment of that life.

The son, Svetaketu, then asked for knowledge about what happened to a man when he went to sleep. Uddhalaka's reply to this question was as follows:

> During sleep we become, for a time as it were, one with the eternal spirit. In the same way as an animal tethered to a peg can go only round and round that central peg but cannot get away from it, the mind of man can only hover about the inner vital breath of Prana. This Prana again is centred round the all-pervading eternal spirit. That spirit and thyself, O Svetaketu! are one and the same.

This last teaching was a bit terse and abstruse to the young listener, who, therefore, prayed for further elucidation of the same. The teacher, in response to the request, continued as follows:

> The honey gathered from various flowers by the bees is put into their hive. The moment it is deposited in the bee-hive, the particle of honey loses its individuality of association with the particular flower in which it was originally secreted. Likewise, the individual soul in a living being loses its individuality of having been of say, a lion, a tiger, a mouse, a worm or a man, and eventually merges in the one only Supreme Being. That Being and thyself are one, O Svetaketu!
>
> So long as the waters of a river flow in that river itself, we can identify them as belonging to that particular river. When these very waters eventually join the sea, their individuality is lost beyond recognition and their merging into the waters of the sea is complete. Even so with the vital breath of the individual being when it coalesces with the Eternal Supreme Being. That Being and thyself are one and the same, my dear son!
>
> We may harm a tree by cutting its roots or dismembering some of its branches, but the tree lives on. Likewise, even if the individual dies, its life persists and this is due to the Eternal

Spirit. That Supreme Being and thyself are one and the same, O Svetaketu!

All these teachings were enlightening and very interesting to the student who listened to these with rapt attention. Still he needed further clarification. Hence, he asked his father to tell him how the unknowable Atman (Supreme Being) was to be comprehended. The learned father satisfied his son's curiosity in the following remarkable way:

Father: You see that spreading banyan tree (Ficus bengalensis) yonder. Go and fetch one of its fruits and bring it to me.

Son: Here you are, Sire. I have brought a red ripe fruit from that tree.

Father:. Split it into two, my dear boy.

Son: It is done, my dear father.

Father: What is it that you find inside?

Son: Numerous little seeds.

Father: Take out one of those seeds and split it into two.

Son: I have done so.

Father: What do you now see in it?

Son: Nothing, Sire.

Father: It is from this seed that a future banyan tree comes out with all its spreading branches. You cannot, however, see its presence in it now, because that existence is a subtle one. Similarly it is the Eternal Spirit in which the germs of all other creations of the Universe reside. That Supreme Being is thyself, O! my son.

The son then asked how, even if known, the Supreme Being was actually to be realized. The sage Uddhalaka replied as follows:

> If you put some salt into a tumbler of water in the night, then go to sleep and look for it in the morning, you will find that the salt has disappeared. If, however, you taste a little of that water, you find that the salt really exists in that water in an unseen dissolved state. In the same way the Eternal Being exists in and permeates through all the objects of creation. That Being, again, and thyself are one and the same.

Finally the sage expounded in the following manner the method of approach towards that Supreme Being:

> A blindfolded man, stranded in a jungle, will just wander hither and thither, not knowing how precisely to reach his home. If he is allowed to remove the covering of his eyes, he would make judicious inquiries of the passers-by, and find his way home. The

search for the Supreme Being should also be conducted in a similar, regulated manner, instead of aimlessly rambling about. That spirit and thyself, O Svetaketu, my dear son! are one and the same.

Thus ended the preaching of Uddhalaka Aruni to his son, Svetaketu.

YAJNYAVALKYA-MAITREYI*

Yajnyavalkya was a great exponent of Brahmavidya. He is described as a preceptor of the king Janak of Mithila. This story reveals victory of spiritualism over materialism, which was one of the prominent bases of the educational system prevailing during that period. This very value tenet is regarded as the main theme of our culture during the present time also. Materialism was considered as means only and not the end in itself particularly for maintaining peace and harmony in the individual life as well as in society.

Of the two wives of the celebrated Vedic seer, Yajnyavalkya, Maitreyi and Katyayani, the former was a brahmavadini or a real seeker after truth, while the latter was of the usual humdrum sort of a typical Hindu wife whose devotion was only to her husband, her household duties and connected matters. The great sage had spent a long enough time as a grihastha or householder. He then thought of entering into the fourth stage of a Hindu Brahmin's life by renouncing the world and becoming a sanyasi (or recluse). He announced his decision to his wife Maitreyi and expressed his intention, as a step prior to becoming an anchorite, to have his mundane belongings partitioned between his two wives before leaving his home.

While Katyayani meekly accepted the proposal, the spiritually-minded Maitreyi's reaction was strange. She said that material wealth was of no avail to her and that, therefore, she would prefer to be taught the ways and means as to how to attain immortality, a consummation which mere riches could not bring. The sage agreed with her that all that wealth could do was to make its possessor happy in the sense of enjoyment of worldly pleasures and comforts but that it could not give one immortality. At this Maitreyi became more insistent on learning about the means to attain immortality. The husband was pleased at this attitude of his wife. He drew her to his side and affectionately started his preaching. He said to her as follows:

---

* Shanti, Ch.305, 306, 307, Sabha 30. 34-35, Satpath Brahman, Yajnyavalkya Smriti.

> The wife loves the husband, not for the sake of the husband, but the husband is dear to the wife only for the sake of the inner atman or soul in the husband which is also the same soul of the wife herself. Likewise, it is not for the sake of the wife that the wife is dear to the husband, but it is for the sake of the inner atman in the wife that the wife is dear to the husband. The same is the case with the children. The children are dear to the parents, not for the sake of the children, but it is for the sake of the atman in the children that they are dear to the parents. Our liking for the Gods, the worlds, and even for the Vedas, is, in the same way, actuated only by our love of the atman which we seek to realize through them.
>
> It is thus only the atman or the inner self of things that we should really care to see, hear, think about, contemplate upon and eventually know. When this is known everything else will be automatically known also.

Then the sage sought the help of similes to propound his teachings to his dear wife and continued as follows :

> When someone sounds a drum, the sound waves caused by it and travelling in the air cannot be caught by anyone and controlled, but when the drum itself is taken possession of, we control everything that comes from it. Thus when the atman is known, everything else in the world that emanates from it is automatically known.
>
> Fire lit by fuel, which is not completely dry, gives rise to copious smoke which issues out in all directions and in the same way, from the one Supreme Being everything else in the world like the Vedas, the Puranas, the histories, the arts and sutras or aphorisms arise.
>
> In the same way as all the waters of the world eventually empty themselves into the sea, even as all external phenomena are known through the sense organs of sight, smell, hearing, touch and taste, even as the mind conceives all ideas, the Spirit knows all.
>
> Completeness and perfection are features of the Spirit. There is no inside or outside to it. It shines of its own accord.
>
> There is a view that with death the human soul also perishes.

When the sage came to this point in his teachings and was about to rebut the last-mentioned view, his wife, Maitreyi, said that it was just that mystery of life and death that she had been longing to know about. The sage then continued his teaching as under :

The view stated above is wrong. The soul does not die. It has neither birth nor death. Its life is unbroken. When the body dies, the soul gets liberated from it and becomes the one and only Being. When there is a duality, one can see the other, one can hear the other, one can speak to the other, and one can think of the other. When, however, there is One Being. One without a second, who can see what, who can hear whom, who can speak to whom and who can think of whom? That One Being is the Atman or the Supreme Soul. He being the Knower of all, how and by what means can He be known?

So saying, the sage departed for his life as an ascetic in the forests.

Appendix V

SATYAKAMA

It is a story which reveals that a man can learn a lot through communion with nature. Satyakama wandering in woods while taking around the herd of cattle of his preceptor realized that the whole neighborhood, entire natural phenomena became his teachers and revealed to him the great reality of the Universe. In the modern educational trend such phenomena is known as "Environmental Education", which is much stressed upon these days through various outdoor activities.

Satyakama, a young lad of the Vedic days, was an aspirant for the knowledge of the Reality. For that purpose he had to seek a guru (preceptor), stay with the latter for a time as celibate (brahmachari) and learn the sacred texts under him. The guru was bound to ask for the boy's spiritual lineage (or Gotra) including his immediate parentage before accepting the latter as his disciple. Hence the boy went to his mother (he not having a father, or, having had one as he certainly should have had, not knowing anything about him) and asked her to tell him his Gotra. Now this question was a little inconvenient to his mother, because he had been born to her out of wedlock when she was roaming about in the jungles during her youth and had committed an act of indiscretion. Nevertheless she realized that she should give her son some reply to enable him to seek the knowledge he was after. She, therefore, simply said that she was herself blissfully ignorant of their Gotra, and that all she knew was that the boy's name was Satyakama and that her own name was Jabala. She, therefore, suggested the boy present himself before any preceptor of his choice under the simple name of Satyakama Jabala, meaning that he was born of a mother known as Jabala.

Satisfied with this reply, the youngster left for the hermitage of a teacher. The guru who was thus approached was known as Haridrumata Gautama. On reaching his would-be preceptor's presence, the young lad made the obeisance usual for the occasion and then mentioned his prayer—that he desired to learn from that personage the sacred texts. The sage put the customary question about the young boy's Gotra. Satyakama then repeated to the sage all the details of the conversation he had with his mother and finally introduced himself merely as Satyakama Jabala, as instructed by his mother. The sage was astonished but was very pleased with the boy's frankness and devotion to truth. And, saying that such scrupulous truth-telling in spite of its unsavoury nature could be the virtue of only one born of a Brahmin father, he accepted the boy as his disciple and asked him to prepare himself for the initiation as a brahmachari (celibate) prior to the commencement of the studies.

The initiation ceremony over, Satyakama became a regular inmate of the sage's hermitage (ashram). But the boy had a hard time there, because of the fastidiousness of the guru. One of the tasks set by the teacher to the young student was that the latter should take into the jungle a herd of four hundred cows, all lean and lanky, and, bring them back as a larger herd of a thousand heads of the same. Satyakama went out as directed. In the jungle he was looking after the animals in his charge. Still the desire for knowledge was burning in him. He, therefore, sought for it by looking for "books in the running brooks", "sermons in stones" and by learning from everything his eyes met. He saw the knowledge of the ultimate Reality his mind was yearning for, even in the sun, the moon and the stars of the heavens.

Once in the midst of the surrounding solitude it occurred to him that all the four corners of the world which lay before his sight should indeed, be all parts of the same great Reality of the Universe. Just then an old bull from among the herd of cattle he was tending said to him that he was right in thinking so. The whole neighbourhood became as it were, his teachers. The flame that issued from the fire he lit during the night when all the animals in his herd had fallen asleep seemed to teach him the same lesson. The moon and the stars over his head also taught him the same fundamental truth about all these phenomena being a part of Brahman or the ultimate Reality.

With the break of day the morning sun appeared and, at its sight, the dew on the flowers disappeared. As the day wore on, the midday sun with its scorching rays was sucking the water from the leaves of trees. In the evening the setting sun appeared before him in all its resplendent glory. All these happenings in nature also told him the same story of their being all parts of the one ultimate Reality called Brahman. His mind was thus suffused with the thought of the Brahman which and only which he saw manifested in everything around him including his own heart-beat. At that juncture the chief among his cattle came to him and announced that the herd had now grown to a thousand in number and that he might, therefore drive them back to his teacher. Satyakama did accordingly.

The guru was pleased to see his disciple back after such a long time.

The effulgence in the student's face surprised the learned guru, who realized from that appearance that the young disciple had learnt about Brahman. Knowing that no human being could have been available in the forest to impart this supreme knowledge to Satyakama, he asked him who it was that had taught him all that knowledge. Satyakama meekly replied that, though it was through communion with nature, it was all only due to the grace of the guru himself. The disciple then requested his teacher for further knowledge and the sage readily obliged seeing that the young man was then fully mature to receive such knowledge.

Thus was fulfilled the desire of young Satyakama to know the ultimate Reality of the Universe.

Appendix VI

GLOSSARY WITH BIOGRAPHICAL NOTES

Angira : Father of Brihaspati, who is known as preceptor of gods. Angira is said to be the third son of Brahma. He is counted as one of the seven Rishis (Saptarishis) Angira's wife's name was Subha, who gave birth to fifteen children, seven sons, including Brihaspati, and eight daughters.

Aasuri : Aasuri is mentioned in the Mahabharata as a great scholar of Yoga. From "Kapil-Aasuri Conversation" we come to know that Aasuri learnt Yoga from Kapil. He was a great ritualist also.

Aksha Krida : Game of dice, a sort of gambling.

Agadtantra : Toxicology, science of poison.

Arthashastra : Political science, Dand Niti. Name of a treatise on the subject compiled by Kautilya (Vishnu Gupta Chanakya), called Arth Vidya also. In Chhandogya it is described as "Nidhi Vidya" (see dialogue between Narada and Sanatkumar).

Ashwa Vidya : Horse-lore, known as Hayayurveda also.

Ashwa Lakshana : Art of diagonizing diseases of horses on the basis of various symptoms; one of 84 Vidyas.

Ashwa-Chikitsa : A name of treatise on horse-lore by Nakul, one of the Pandavas.

Ashwini Kumar : Divine twin physicians.

Ashtavakra : Scholar son of Kahod Muni and compiler of "Ashtavakra Geeta".

Aayurvidya : Science of life, ancient Indian system of medicine.

Acharyas : Expounders of a system of philosophy; preceptors.

Asuras : Demons. They were divine beings but, as opposed to the gods, they were generally evil. They frequently fought with the gods, or troubled human beings. They lived in underground worlds or in forests.

Avatar : An incarnation of God, generally of Vishnu. God is said to take birth on earth either in human or animal form whenever the need arises, for the destruction of evil in the world or for establishing Dharma.

Aditi : Mother of the deities.

Agneya : A missile emitting fire

Anasuya : Wife of a sage named Atri.

Ayodhya : Capital of Koshala.

Amba : The eldest daughter of the king of Kashi.

Ambalika : The youngest daughter of the king of Kashi; married to Vichitravirya.

Ambika : The younger daughter of the king of Kashi; married to Vichitravirya.

Arjuna : The son of Pandu and Kunti; one of the five Pandavas.

Ashwasena : The son of Takshaka; a snake.

Bharadwaj : Bhardwaj was a son of Brihaspati and Mamta. He was deserted by his parents and brought up by a king, Bharat. Later on he became heir-apparent to Bharata's throne. This story is interwoven in Matsyapurana. In Mahabharata Bhardwaj is described as one of the seven sages and as a priest to King Bharat. By the grace of his priest (Bhardwaj) the King was blessed with a son named "Upmanyu". Thus the sage described in Matsyapuran is different from the one described in Mahabharata. One Bhardwaj directed Rama, during exile to the path leading towards Chitrakoot and advised him to stay over there peacefully.

Babhruvahana : The son of Arjuna by Chitrangada.

Balarama : The elder brother of Krishna.

Bhagadatta : The king of Pragjyotisha.

Bhima : The second son of Pandu and Kunti; one of the Pandavas.

Bhishma : The son of Shantanu and Ganga; called Pitamaha (Grandfather).

Brihannalaa : The name adopted by Arjuna at Viratanagar.

Brihaspati : Brihaspati, son of Angira sage, was a great preceptor of gods (Suras). He has his own school of followers. Kautilya in his "Arthashastra" has quoted opinions of Brihaspati on many aspects of statecraft. He was a great exponent of "Dandneeti".

Brahmacharin : One belonging to the first Ashrama; student devoted to the practice of spiritual discipline, a celibate belonging to the first stage of life.

Baadarayan Samhita : The Mahabharata being regarded as the fifth Veda. Another name of Vyas was Baadarayan Vyas. Therefore, Mahabharata is called "Baadarayan Samhita".

Bhrigu : Famous expounder of Astrology, described as ancient discoverer of fire. He was one of the seven mind-born sons of Brihma. According to Vishnu Puran there are nine Brahmarishis—Bhrigu, Pulastya, Pulah, Kratu, Angiras, Marichi, Daksha, Atri and Vashishtha. These Brahmarishis are also called Prajapatis (Lords of off spring) in Hindu mythology. Mahabharata gives a legend of Bhrigu cursing Indra. The Indra of that age, named Nahusha, being filled with pride, lost the benefit of his previous good works, and in his presumption caused the rishis to carry him about.

Brahmastra : A divine weapon, said to be given by Lord Brahma. This is said to be the most powerful of all divine weapons.

Brahmana : The priestly caste of Hindu society. Teachers were also drawn from this class.

Brahma, Vishnu, Mahesh (Siva) : These are the three aspects of the one God, just like three fibres entwined into a single rope. These three aspects of God are said to be instrumental in the creation, sustenance and destruction of the Universe respectively. But these functions are not watertight. For example, Siva is sometimes referred to as the origin of the Universe.

Bharatas : Descendants of King Bharata who was an illustrious ancestor of Shantanu, and who ruled at Hastinapur. Our country "Bharat Varsha" is named after King Bharata. Bharata was the son of Dushyanta and Shakuntala.

Bhishma : A son of Shantanu and half-brother of Krishna Daipaayan Vyas, compiler of Mahabharata. He was the grandfather of Pandavas and a great warrior, statesman and scholar of his time. His birth-name was Devavrit. He is referred to in "Artha-shastra" as "Kaunapdant'. Kautilya has quoted his views on various aspect of statecraft particularly on the appointment of ministers. He conducted the government of Hastinapur in the name of Pandavas during their minority. Education of Pandava princes was entrusted to him. Dronacharya was appointed by him for educating the Pandava and Kaurava princes. In Shanti and Anushasan Parvan his exhortion given to Yudhishthir on various duties of a king is a master piece in the history of state-craft. He fought in Mahabharata war for ten days as the Commander-in-Chief of Kaurava army. He was an excellent warrior and a model for warlike kings.

Chakra : (Sudarshan-Chakra)—A divine weapon shaped like a shining golden disc. This is Lord Vishnu's weapon. As Krishna was an incarnation of Vishnu, it was also Lord Krishna's weapon.

Chitrangada : The elder son of Shantanu and Satyavati.

Chitrangada : The princess of Manipur; the wife of Arjuna.

Chitra Shastra : Drawing and Painting. Other names of the lore are : Chitra-Vidya, Chitrakala, Chitra-lakshan, etc. King Nagnajit is said to be the expounder of this lore, who is described in Mahabharata as a disciple of Prahlad and grand-father of Shakuni and Gandhari (See Adi Parvan, Ch.63).

Durvasa : A sage, son of Atri and Ansuya

Dushana : A rakshasa killed by Rama.

Devas : Gods. These were divine beings but, as opposed to the asuras or demons, they were good. They lived in heaven, on the top of the mythical Mount Meru (also called Sumeru).

Devavrata : The name of Ganga's son by Shantanu; Bhishma.

Damagranthi : The name adopted by Nakula at Virata Nagar.

Dhananjaya : One of the many names of Arjuna.

Dhaumya : The priest of the Pandavas.

Dhrishtadyumna : The son of Drupada; brother of Draupadi.

Dhritarashtra : The son of Ambika; blind ruler of Hastinapur; father of Duryodhana; brother of Pandu.

Draupadi : The daughter of Drupada, King of Panchala; the wife of the five Pandavas.

Dronacharya : Drona was preceptor of Pandava princes. He is also known as Drona Bhardwaj. Drona had received training in various arms and archery from Agniwesh and Bhaargava Parshuram. Drona was fellow-pupil of Drupad, father of Draupadi. Later on when Drupad became king he insulted Drona who in turn defeated Drupad with the help of Pandavas and wrested half of his kingdom.

Gargya : A priest of Bharata's maternal uncle, Yudhajit

Gautama : A great sage, husband of Ahalya.

Gayatri : (i) A sacred verse of the Vedas.
(ii) The deity of that sacred verse.

Ganapati : Also called Ganesha. According to Hindu mythology, the elephant-headed son of God Siva and Parvati. Prayer to Him overcomes all obstacles. He is the god of wisdom and good fortune. Being prayed by Vyas he acceded to his prayer to become his scribe to write down Mahabharata.

Ganga (The Ganges) : The chief of the sacred streams of India, whose waters are said to have the power of cleansing all past, present, and future sins. It is believed to be divine. The account of her birth and appearance on earth forms an interesting episode in the Ramayana. The story is told to Rama by hermit Vishvamitra as he was travelling with Rama and his brother Lakshmana.

Guru-dakshina : The fee voluntarily paid by the disciple to his guru when his studies are completed.

Gandharvas : A class of semi-divine beings who are the musicians of the gods.

Garuda : A giant bird, devotee and vehicle of Lord Vishnu.

Gawopnishad : A term given in Mahabharata for "Govidya". Agni Purana describes it as "Gawayurveda" (Ch. 292).

Gandharva : Semi-gods like Chitraratha, Tumbru, etc. (see Sabha Parvan).

Gandharva-vidya : It includes like vocal and instrumental music, dance, etc. Narad is said to be the expounder of Gandharva-vidya.

Gita : The famous philosophical classic of 700 verses, contained in the Mahabharata. The whole of the spiritual philosophy of the Hindus is briefly given here as the instruction of Sri Krishna to Arjuna on the battle-field of Kurukshetra. (Udyog Parvan, Ch.23-40)

Grihasthasram : Married life as a householder. The second of the four Asramas ending in Sanyasa.

Hidimbi : The sister of Hidimba; married to Bhima.

Hidimba : A demon killed by Bhima.

Ikshwaka : A forefather of Rama.

Indra : King of the gods. Since he made greater sacrifices than them, Indra had gained supremacy over the other gods and become their king. He is the god who commands the rains too fall and make earth fruitful.

Jaigishavya : He was fellow pupil of Panchshikha. He is referred to the Mahabharata as a great scholar of Yoga Vidya.

Jamdagni : Father of Parsuram and son of Richeek Jamdagni's mother's name was Satyavati. Satyavati was the sister of a great sage Vishwamitra, a son of Gadhi, a great king of his time.

Janamejaya : The son of Parikshita and great grandson of Arjuna and grandson of Abhimanyu.

Jayadratha : The king of the Sindhus; married to Dushshala; the sister of Duryodhana.

Kaashyap : Kaashyap was a famous toxicologist. He is referred to in "Kaashyap-Takshak episode" of Mahabharata. While going to Hastinapur to save the life of Parikshit whose death was predicted due to snake-bite. Influenced by his magical power of Mantra, Takshaka requested him to desist from going to Hastinapur to save the king's life. Allured by the handsome amount of wealth offered by Takshaka he acceded to request and returned home clearing the way for Takshaka to fulfil his mission (death of Parikshit).

Kanva : In Mahabharata we find a charming description of Kanva's hermitage. Dushyant had seen Shakuntala in his hermitage only. Kanva's name appears in the Rigveda and other Vedic literature. Kanva belonged to the family of Angiras. In ancient literature we find many sages named 'Kanva' such as Kanva Narshad, Kanva Shrayas, Kanva ghor, Medhatithi Kanva, etc. But the one related to "Shankuntala Episode" was Kaashyap Kanva. He belonged to Kashyap-clan and as such used to be called "Kaashyap" also.

Kavi : In ancient Hindu literature including Mahabharata it stands for a learned person, still now great physicians are attributed as "Kaviraj". In Mahabharata Kavi is used as an attribute for Shukracharya, Vidur, etc.

Kavya-kriya : Versification, being a process of composing poems, one of 64 arts mentioned in the Kama-stura.

Kaunap-danta : Another name of Bhishma, referred to in the Artha-shastra of Kautilya.

Kapila : The sage, who is the propounder of the Sankhya System.

Karma : Rite; act; the result of all past actions.

Karma Kanda : Ritual section (of the Vedas); the Brahmana portion.

Krishna : Lord Krishna was an incarnation of Vishnu who took birth to destroy evil in the world.

Koshala : A province of ancient India, with Ayodhya as its capital.

Kritvarma : A cousin of Krishna; fought on the side of Duryodhana.

Kunti : The daughter of Sura; married to Pandu; the mother of Karna and the five Pandavas.

Karna : Born to Kunti during her virginity. For fear of censure by relatives she deserted him exposing in a river. The child was found by Adhirath, a charioteer, and nurtured by his wife Radha. Hence he was afterward called Radhey, though named as Vasushena by his foster-parents. Lord Indra conferred upon him enormous strength and changed his name to Karna. He is also called Vaikranta, being the son of Vikranta (the Sun). Duryodhana made him the king of Anga territory and as he was extremely loyal to the Kauravas. After Bhishma and Drona he was appointed as commander-in-chief of the Kaurava army. He fought and led the army very efficiently for two days; but lastly he was deceitfully slain by Arjuna at the behest of Lord Krishna. He was born clothed in armour. His glory is still alive specially for his undaunted bravery and matchless generosity.

Maarich Kashyap : One of the seven sons of Brahma was Marichi. Being son of Marichi, Kashyap was called Marichi Kashyap. Kashyapa's other name was Aristhnemi. He is said to be a great scholar of science of medicine (Ayurveda). His famous treatise on Ayurveda is "Kaashyap Samhita". He established his hermitage at Haridwar. Jeevak, a famous physician of the Buddhist period, is said to be a disciple of Kashyap.

Madri : The wife of Pandu and the mother of Nakula and Sachadeva.

Markandeya : A noted sage who narrated instructive stories to Yudhishthira.

Maya : Maya is referred in Mahabharata as a great architect who built celestial Yajnyamandap for Yudhishthir, who performed a celebrated Rajsuya Yajnya. An elaborate description of this Yajnya is available in Sabha Parvan of Mahabharata. Maya is referred in the Ramayana also as father of Mandodari, a principal queen of Ravana. Maya was perhaps the contemporary of Vishvakarma.

Mritsanjivani Vidya : A lore by which the dead ones can be restored to life. Acharya Shukra was the expounder of this lore, who used to bring back the dead demons to life. Now only the Mantra is available but the identification of the particular herb is lost (see Bhishma Parvan, Ch.71).

Mallvidya : Lore of wrestling. In Mahabharata there is an interesting account of famous wrestlers like Bhima, Jarasandha, Musti, Chanur, etc.

Narada : Narada is a mythological figure, who is often described in the epics and elsewhere as the messenger of the gods, and imparting information that was only known to them. It was he who persuaded the sons of Daksha not to beget offspring and who was cursed for his interference. It was Narada, who informed Kansa of the approaching birth of Krishna, which led that king to slay the children of Vasudeva. Therefore, his common name is Kalikaaraka, the strife-maker. In subsequent literature he is described as a spy and marplot. The nomenclature "Narada" is frequently employed as a term of abuse and used to describe a quarrelsome, meddling person. But he was a wise diplomat, highly skilled in arts and arms, an eloquent messenger of the gods, either to one another or to the favoured mortals. He was a great musician of exquisite skill. The credit for invention of "Veena" (Indian lute) goes to him. He was the most favoured and staunch devotee of Lord Vishnu. In Mahabharata Narada figures as a religious teacher whereas "Uttar Kand" of the Ramayana is a specimen of his teaching. It was Narada, who narrated the life of Rama to Valmiki and advised him to depict the character of Rama in versical form, which was accomplished with the grace of Brahma.

Parasurama : Long ago, when the Kshatriyas were getting too proud and arrogant on account of their strength, Lord Vishnu took birth as a human to teach them a lesson. He took form as Parasurama, son of the Brahman sage Jamadagni, and grew up to be a great warrior. One day, when Parasurama had gone into the forest, some Kshatriya princes went to Jamadagni's ashrama and killed him. When Parasurama returned to the ashrama and saw what had happened, he took a vow that he would wipe out the Kshatriya race from the face of the earth to avenge the killing of his father. Adopting as his weapons the battle-axe and the bow, the mighty warrior waged war on the Kshatriyas twentyone times till the lakes were filled with blood and the rivers ran red. But Parasurama himself became proud and arrogant on account of his victories, but his pride was finally subdued by Sri Rama as described in the Ramayana.

Pracheta : Valmiki's father.

Purochan : A friend of Duryodhan; constructed the wax palace.

Pitra Vidya : Details of performing Shraddha. It includes calling

	and entertaining of spirits also. The latter one is called "Pret Vidya" also. In modern terminology it is covered under "Para-psychology". More specifically it may be called "Pitra-Pret Vidya".
Puran Vidya	: A branch of learning which deals with genealogical and mythological accounts of various kings and deities. In ancient Hindu literature these puranas are treated on a par with history. The Mahabharata is considered "Itihas" and "Puran" both.
Panchshikha	: He is referred to in Mahabharata as a great scholar of the Samkhya system of Indian philosophy. In Shanti parvan (Sec. XII) of Mahabharata we have a detailed account of his views on the Samkhya system. In "Sulbha-Janak Conversation" Janak recalls him as his preceptor, whom he was indebted to for his profound knowledge of Samkhya and Yoga.
Radha	: A wife of Adhirath who brought up Karna.
Rasatala	: One of the seven lower strata of this cosmic unit.
Rishyashringa	: A sage and priest who performed a song-giving ritual for King Dasharatha; son of Vibhandaka.
Raj-dharma	: Other synonyms are : Dand Niti, Raj-shastra and Artha-shastra. The treatises on political theories and practical governance were originally called Nand-Niti or Artha-shastra. In Shanti and Anushasan Parvan (Sec. XII and XIII) of Mahabharata, we come across a detailed and quite elaborate account of various aspects of Raj-dharma, exhorted by Bhishma to Yudhishthir.
Rajasuyayagya	: During ancient times when a king wanted to take the title of "emperor" he performed a Rajasuya sacrifice. A spirited horse was set free for a year, to roam at will over various other kingdoms. It was constantly followed by the army of its owner king. If any king challenged the authority of the aspirant king, he tried to capture the horse and a battle followed. If, at the end of the year, the horse was still free, its owner performed a sacrifice during which he was crowned Emperor.
Satyavati	: The wife of Shantanu; the mother of Chitrangada and Vichitravirya; also the mother of Vyasa.

Shakuni : The maternal uncle of Duryodhana.

Shikhandin : Amba born as the daughter of Drupada; half-male warrior.

Subhadraa : The sister of Krishna; married to Arjuna.

Shalihotra : He is referred in the first and second sections of Mahabharata. He was a great scholar of horse-lore. Pandavas had visited his hermitage along with Hidimba, a wife of Bhima. There are many treatises on horse-lore to his credit, which include "Shalihotra Samhita", "Ashvalakshan Shastra," etc.

Shukracharya : He was the preceptor and priest of demons, and blind in one eye. He is said to have possessed the power of raising the dead. Devayani, the daughter of Shukra, was deeply in love with Kacha, a son of Brihaspati and a pupil of his father, who had been to Shukra for the express purpose of learning from him the incantation for raising the dead. After having undergone many odd trials ultimately Kacha succeeded in his mission. Other nomenclatures for Shukra are Ushana, Kavya, Kavi, Bhargava, Daityaguru, etc. He was a great scholar of statecraft. "Dand Neeti" was the title adopted by Ushnas and "Artha-shastra" by Brihaspati, for their respective works on statecraft, which were very famous in Hindu classical times.

Sairandhri : When the Pandavas were living in the terra incognita for a year in the palace of Virata, Draupadi became companion and attendant to a princess and her disguised name was Sairandhri.

Swayamvara : A ceremony held by the Hindu kings of ancient India. Eligible princes were invited to this ceremony so that a princes could select a husband of her own choice from among them.

Tamasa : A river near Valmiki's cottage.

Tara : Bali's wife.

Tantripal : The name adopted by Sahadeva in Viratnagar.

Trijata : A good-natured lady attending upon Sita in Ashoka-vatika.

Upanishad : The part of the Vedas dealing with the highest philosophical speculations and institutional knowledge of reality.

Uttaraa : The daughter of King Virata; married to Abhimanyu.

Uttara Kumara : The youngest son of Virata.

Vashistha : Vashistha, a famous sage, is referred to in the Ramayana as well as in Mahabharata. In the Ramayana he is described as a preceptor of Ikshwaku clan and as a chief counsellor and spiritual guide of Dasharatha. In Mahabharata also we find "Vaishastha-Janak Conversation". One Vashistha is described as a father of Parashar and grandfather of Krishna Dvaipayan Vyas. One Vashistha is described as one of the seven sons of Brahma. Thus there were many sages called "Vashistha" by name. Vashishtha mentioned in the Ramayana must be different from the one described in Mahabharata.

Vichitravirya : One of the two sons of Shantanu and Satyavati.

Vaarta-shastra : Being a collective term for agriculture, trade and commerce, one of the three original lores. Other counterparts are Trayee and Danda Niti.

Vedanta : Literally "end of the Vedas". The religious philosophy which emerged in India towards the end of the Vedic period.

Vidur : Vidur was an incarnation of Lord Dharma. He was unparalleled in statesmanship and knowledge of Dharma. He was chief counsellor to Dhritrashtra. His teachings are enshrined in Mahabharata in the form of "Vidur Neeti".

Visvakarma : Tvastri, or, as he is called in later works, Vishvakarma, was the most outstanding architect and workman of the gods—the Hindu Vulcan. The heavenly palaces were built by him, and the warlike gods are indebted to him for their wonder-working weapons. "Pushpak plane" originally owned by Kuber was made by Vishwakarma. The plane was, later on, snatched away by Ravana. After being victor, Rama used this very Pushpak plane for returning to Ayodhya. In Mahabharata Prajapati Twashtri and divine architect Vishwakarma are mentioned as identical. When Trishira, son of Twashtri, was killed by Lord Indra, Twashtri underwent severe penances to get another son named

Vritra, who was bent upon taking revenge on Indra. To kill his own son (Vritra) in the interest of the nation he made famous weapon of Indra called "Vajra". Besides Vajra he is said to be the maker of many divine weapons including Trishul, Sudarshan Chakra, etc. Thus Vishwakarma was the most outstanding architect.

Vyas : Parashar, a sage, met Satyavati as he was crossing the river Yamuna and Vyas was the result. He was born on an island of the river and as such was called Dwaipayan (one who moves on an island) is said to have been the arranger of the Vedas, the compiler of Mahabharata and the Puran, and the founder of Vedanta system of philosophy.

After the death of his half-brother Vichitravirya he married childless widows—Ambika and Ambalika at the command of his mother Satyavati and produced Dhritrashtra from Ambika, Pandu from Ambalika and Vidur from a maid-servant of Ambalika. After fulfilling mother's commands, Vyas returned to his ascetic life in the forest.

Yajnavalkya : A Rishi in the Brihadaranyakopanishad who expounds Brahman to King Janak and his own wife Maitreyi. Yajnavalkya is described as a champion in various tournaments on Brahma Vidya particularly in the Chhandogya Upnishad.

Yoga : An ancient Hindu method of physical and mental self-control, the ultimate aim of which is to re-unite the practitioner with the Supreme Being.

Yudhishthir : The eldest of five Pandava princes. He is said to be a son of Dharma, virtue. He is the Hindu ideal of excellence—a pattern of justice, calm, passionless composure, chivalrous honour and cold heroism. He is described as having a majestic lion-like gait, with a Wellington-like profile and long lotus-eyes.

Bibliography

The Mahabharata (Critical Edition), BORI, Pune.

Ancient Indian Historical Traditions : F.E. Pargiter, Oxford, 1922.

Ancient Indian Education, R.K. Mukherjee, Varanasi.

An Outline of the Religious Literature of India: J.N. Farquhar, London, 1920.

Buddhist India: Rhys Devis.

"Bhargvangiras Elements in Mahabharata": Shende, Poona, 1940, (thesis), BORI.

Catalogus Catalogorum, An Alphabetical Register of Sanskrit Works and Authors: Theodor Aufrecht, 3 Volumes (1891, 1896 and 1903).

Encyclopaedia of Literature : Cassal's.

Catalogue of Sanskrit manuscripts in Private Libraries of Gujrat, Kathiawad, Karanchi, Sindha and Khandesh: G. Buhler, Fescicle I, 1871.

Contribution to a Bibliography of Indian Art and Aesthetics: Haridas Mitra, Shanti Niketan.

Dictionary of Hindu Architecture; P.K. Acharya

Epic India: C.V. Vidya, Bombay, 1907.

Encyclopaedia of Religion and Ethics: Ed. by James Hastings, Vol. I, T. & T. Chark, Ẹdinburg, 1965.

Great Epic of India: Hopkins.

Geographical and Economic Studies in the Mahabharata, Upayan Parvan, Dr. Motichandra, Varanasi.

Hindu Polity: K.P. Jayaswal, 4th Edn. Bangalore, 1967.

History of Sanskrit Poetics: P.V. Kane, Motilal Benarsidas, 2nd Edn. 1961.

History of Sanskrit Literature : Arthur A. Macdonell, London, 1925 (Abridged Edition also) published at Delhi, 1961.

History of Indian Literature : Winternitz, Vol. 1-2.

History of Indian Chemistry : P.C. Roy Krishna, Dr. Bhagwandas, BVB, Bombay.

History of Dharmshashtra: P.V. Kane, Vol. 1-5, BORI, Pune.

India: As Known to Panini, Dr. V.S. Agarwala, Varanasi.

Index to the names in the Mahabharat (in 3 volumes): Saurrenson, London, 1904-1924 (Indian Ed. published in 1972).

Studies in Indian Art: Dr. V.S. Agarwala, Varanasi.

Studies in the Puranic Records of Hindu Rites and Customs: H.C. Hazra, Dacca, 1940.

Studies in the Epics and Puranas: A.D. Pusalkar, Bharatiya Vidya Bhavan, Bombay, (1st edn.), 1963.

Sexual Life in Ancient India: J.J. Mayer, London, 2 Vols., 1930.

Sankhya and Yoga: Richard Garbe.

The Mahabharata: A Critique: C.V. Vaidya, Delhi, 1966.

The Sankhya System: Keith.

The Vedasthan or the Ancient Home of Indo-Aryans: T.J. Kedar, Nagpur.

Vaishnavism, Shaivism and other Minor Religious Systems: Dr. R.G. Bhandarkar.

Value Education : Theory and Practice, Dr. N.L. Gupta, Krishna Brothers, Ajmer, 1986.

Values and Creativity, Dr. N.L. Gupta, Arya Book Depot, New Delhi, 1992.

Index